Caring for Creation

**The environmental crisis:
A Canadian Christian
call to action**

David G. Hallman

Wood Lake
Books
inc

Cover photo and design: Tim Faller
Editing: Jim Taylor, Tim Faller

Canadian Cataloguing in Publication Data

Hallman, David G.
  Caring for Creation

ISBN 0-919599-73-3
  1. Pollution. 2. Environmental protection.
3. Man—influence on nature. 4. Christian
ethics. I. Title.
TD170.H34 1989   363.7   C89-091461-3

Published by
Wood Lake Books Inc.,
Box 700, Winfield, BC, Canada, V0H 2C0

Printed in Canada by
Friesen Printers
Altona, MB, R0G 0B0

Table of Contents

"To see the world in a grain of sand
And Heaven in a wild flower,
To hold eternity in your hand
And Heaven in an hour."

William Blake
"Auguries of Innocence"

Acknowledgments

I had the privilege for about five years to work with a national committee of the United Church of Canada responsible for issues related to energy and the environment. I greatly respect the commitment and dedication of its members to preserving the fragile planet earth. They provided inspiration for this book. Some of them read and gave helpful feedback to early drafts. In particular, I thank Joanne Cag, Susan Holtz, Greg Johnson, Doris Migus, Carmen Milenkovic, and Ray Nash.

Environmental concerns have been a major focus of The Taskforce on the Churches and Corporate Responsibility. I appreciate the opportunity to have been one of the United Church representatives and to have worked with other churches in this ecumenical effort. The Taskforce co-ordinator, Moira Hutchinson, gives sensitive and probing leadership. She brought these same skills to her reviewing of many of my chapters.

I do not have formal theological training. I believe, however, that we all struggle with and can discuss theological issues. Two people who have tried to help me do it with some clarity in this book are Douglas John Hall and Roger Hutchinson. I am grateful to both of them for their comments. Many people around the world, myself included, appreciate Doug's significant contribution to the World Council of Churches' work on the "integrity of creation."

A variety of people from Canadian environmental organizations assisted me through reviewing chapters and/or providing information. I would like to acknowledge the help of John Jackson of the Ontario Toxic Waste Research Coalition, Colin Isaacs from Pollution Probe, Julia Langer, Andrea Prazmowski and Kai Millyard of Friends of the Earth, Michael Perley and Adelle Hurley of the Canadian Coalition on Acid Rain, Carmen Milenkovic of the Inter-Church Uranium Committee, Pat Adams from Probe International, and Norm Rubins of Energy Probe. Lee Holland of the United Church's Division of World Outreach also gave me useful comments on several chapters.

I have received encouragement to write this book from senior staff of the United Church's Division of Mission in Canada for which I work. In particular, I want to thank Bonnie Greene, Howard Brox and Gerry Hopkirk. They expressed their conviction that Canadian Christians are anxious to apply their faith in a concern for the future of creation. They felt this book might help.

Early drafts showed my inexperience in writing. Wood Lake Books' editor, Jim Taylor, helped me focus. In later drafts, he showed me how to say what I wanted more precisely and with fewer words. I am very grateful.

Though these many people provided helpful comments, I, of course, accept responsibility for any errors or inadequacies in the book.

Finally, I dedicate the book to my friend, William Conklin. He has had to put up with my hours at the word processor. He also provided very practical assistance without which I could never have started writing. But more than that, his spiritual concern for the future of the earth and its most vulnerable creatures propels me forward. I see that concern verging on despair sometimes in him and others like him. For him and for them, I write what I hope will be a book with at least a glimmer of hope.

Preface

The world today faces a whole series of environmental crises.
My country, Canada, experiences the effects of many of
these. To save this planet, humanity must learn more about
the problems and find solutions. I have written this book to
help us understand what is happening to our environment and
what we can do about it.

The book is also about the role that Christians can play. I
believe that we can make a positive contribution to the
ecological crises facing our planet. Our faith requires it of us.

I have written this book as an invitation for you to become
involved. Canadians are concerned about environmental
issues; Christians believe that God created and loves the
earth. As Canadian Christians, we have rarely put those two
sides of ourselves together. If we do, we can be a powerful in-
strument for positive change.

You may disagree with some specific points or some
general arguments in this book. That is fine. All I ask is that
you take them seriously.

We can help save the earth. With God. With prayer and
action. With each other.

This book tries to integrate theological reflection about
humanity's relationship to creation with straightforward
descriptions of a range of the environmental problems facing
Canada. Each chapter includes practical suggestions of what
we can do as individuals and groups.

After a general introduction in chapter one, I devote
chapter two to looking at some problems of the past in Christian theology that have contributed to our world's present environmental crises. But I also describe some exciting new
thinking that can help us see our faith as central to finding
solutions to the current destruction of God's creation.

Chapters three to nine provide what I hope is an easily understood overview of some critical environmental issues: acid rain, toxic wastes, the garbage crisis, problems related to uranium mining and nuclear power, destruction of the ozone layer, the climatic warming of the greenhouse effect, and Canadian participation in some of the Third World's ecological disasters. I have tried to condense a great deal of information on each issue, so that you can grasp the essence of the problem without getting overwhelmed by technical details.

But I want to do more than depress you with the seriousness of the environmental crisis. We can all do something to help, so each of the middle chapters contains specific suggestions for action.

The final chapter identifies some major shifts that I believe are necessary if we are to rescue the planet from the destructive course we have set.

Each of the middle chapters focuses on a specific environmental problem. You can select specific issues that you want to pursue individually or discuss in a study group. I encourage you to read the first and last chapters in conjunction with one or more of the middle ones. These two "book end" chapters talk about a vision of how we can relate to creation and to God in a more healthy way. We must develop such a vision if we are to move beyond the overwhelmingness of the problems we face.

I am not an environmental expert. I do not have any formal training in the field. What I share through this book is what I have learned on my own. Some of that has come through being on the national staff of The United Church of Canada, and having the responsibility for providing some leadership within the church on how we can exercise better stewardship of God's creation.

I mention this for a couple of reasons. First, I am no different from most of you who read this. We are not experts. But we do live on this planet together, and we do care about what happens to it. We can teach ourselves what we need to know about the environmental crisis and we can work together to save our environment.

Second, because we are not experts, we may make mistakes from time to time. (Not that the experts are always right either!) I may have made errors in writing this book. Some of my data may not be 100% correct. I have tried very hard to ensure accuracy. But even if there are mistakes, they should not undermine the major theme—that we have some big problems on our hands and we had better solve them soon. In this, we are all learning together: scientists, environmentalists, industry, government, and general public. Our knowledge is never complete, but together we must keep searching for answers and working toward solutions.

A final word. This book deals with what I call the negative side of the environmental crisis. It describes mainly the pollution problems resulting from our present lifestyle. We have to stop this poisoning of the earth, water and air.

However, solving these immediate problems will not guarantee the long-term sustainability of the earth. We have to change the way we make use of the earth's natural resources. This is—or could be—the positive side of our present crisis. We have to learn how to live in a way that does not overuse non-renewable resources and that adapts our practices to being non-destructive to the environment. This means changes in our approach to agriculture, forestry, fisheries, energy development and use, manufacturing, etc.

I point to some of the needed changes in this book, but doing full justice to those issues would require another book. I have chosen to focus on the most urgent crisis issues here. Ultimately, if the earth is to survive, we will have to combine both a solution to the negative aspects (i.e. pollution) and development of the positive side of the environmental crisis (i.e. our use of natural resources).

This may not be enjoyable reading. We can easily get depressed by the environmental destruction that we see around us. But I sincerely hope that by understanding more about these problems and their potential solutions, we will all feel more capable of doing something to make a change. This is intended as an empowering book. You be the judge.

David G. Hallman
Toronto
1989

Canada has an abundance of lakes, but thousands of them no longer support life because of pollution.

Introduction

I live in the Beach neighborhood of Toronto. It is a short walk down the street to the lake. But we cannot swim in the lake. It is too polluted. I'm not sure that we should be drinking the water that comes out of our tap either. It comes from the lake too. There is a high incidence of cancer among some of our long-term neighbors. A garbage incinerator on the waterfront pumped tons of carcinogenic dioxins into the air for decades. The winds blew it over our homes. The soil in the side garden where we grow vegetables may be contaminated. I haven't gotten it tested. Perhaps I'm afraid to find out.

You probably have your own list of environmental fears. Each year they get closer to home.

Thousands of lakes in Canada are dead. All life forms in those lakes have been killed by acid rain. Toxic wastes leak into the sources of drinking water for millions of Canadians. The livelihood of northern native communities is threatened by pollution from paper mills, destruction of the ecology by companies drilling for oil and gas, and uranium mine tailings precariously stored next to waterways.

With the greenhouse effect warming our climate, parts of the prairies may become deserts. The destruction of the ozone layer in the atmosphere will cause the rates of skin cancer to multiply dramatically. Highly toxic chemicals such as PCBs (polychlorinated biphenyls) are stored in warehouses all over the country where a fire would force mass evacuation of the community and threaten the health of those affected. It already happened in Quebec in the summer of 1988. Canada is not immune to industrial accidents like Bhopal in India, Chernobyl in Russia, or the Swiss fire that resulted in tons of toxic chemicals going into the Rhine River.

What is happening to our communities, our country, our earth? Watching the nightly news or reading the paper has become a depressing activity. We Canadians used to live in a relatively comfortable cocoon. We had no wars going on in our land, no major racial tensions, no mass starvation. But the growing destruction of our environment comes much closer to home.

I have little doubt that Canadians care deeply about what happens to the environment. We worry about how pollution damages our air, our water and our land. But when we all have a million things keeping us busy, do we have the time, the energy to do something about these environmental issues? And we wonder, can we as individuals really make a difference? Isn't it up to big companies and government to act?

Many young people are asking a different question. They ask how we can *not* care about pollution. How dare we destroy their future by disregarding the environmental consequences of our present lifestyle?

Those of us who are Christians are faced with another question. What does it mean to have stewardship responsibility for creation?

Serious questions. I'm writing this book to search out some answers. There actually are more answers than we may sometimes think. We do know what causes much of the destruction of the environment. And if we were prepared as a society to do more research, we would know a lot more about the sources of some of our problems.

We are also starting to understand what is necessary to solve these problems. We *can* clean up *some* of our pollution right now. If we considered the environment enough of a priority, we could even find ways of dealing with the more difficult problems. There are technological fixes for some problems, but others will require major changes in how we live and function as a society. Yet these are not great mysteries. We know already much of what will be needed.

There has been some useful theological writing done in the last number of years that can help us better understand what God may have intended for our relationship to the rest of creation. A new vision is needed. Christian theology can help.

Overcoming obstacles to a clean environment

The real obstacles to a clean environment are not technological or scientific. What we lack is the moral will to do something about these problems. We are guilty of the sin of commission in creating the problems, and we are guilty of the sin of omission in not doing more about them.

We use many excuses; some we verbalize, others are less conscious.

Most of us don't often see the results of pollution in our daily lives. We are able to continue our everyday activities relatively unaware of the problems. As long as they do not affect us directly, we feel that we can ignore or avoid them.

Another reason for not dealing with environmental problems is our awe at the beauty and buoyancy of creation itself.

When we view the magnificence and scope of the created order, we are tempted to believe that it could easily withstand the assaults of feeble humanity. The resilience that nature demonstrates, and its ability to recover from a certain amount of pollution, may prove a disadvantage if it distracts us from recognizing the seriousness of the damage we cause.

There are economic complications in trying to address environmental problems. Cleaning up the environment costs money. In some cases, lots of money. Who will pay?

With that goes the issue of jobs. We are reluctant to insist that a company install pollution control equipment if, as they claim, the cost will force them to shut down completely.

We may also find ourselves overwhelmed by the complexity of the issues and prefer just to avoid dealing with them. Although we *know* the causes and solutions to many environmental problems, most solutions would be complex to implement. Solving one problem can cause another.

Along with feeling overwhelmed often comes the reaction of despair. Can anything really be done about all these problems anyway? The problems seem too intractable, the solutions fraught with too many difficulties. We lose hope. We give up trying. We live just for today and abandon the future.

Understanding the vulnerability of the environment

Personally, I can no longer hide behind these kinds of excuses. Over the past few years, I have become aware that the environment is sufficiently fragile that it could be irrevocably damaged by our industrial, agricultural, and consumer practices. I am not alone in this conviction. I believe that many other Canadians will no longer tolerate destruction of the environment either.

We have a feeling about the land and the water. Perhaps it's because our country is so big. Most of us have traveled enough in Canada to have seen the magnificence of different regions—from the rocky coasts of Newfoundland and the Maritimes, through the great forests of northern Quebec and

Ontario, to the wide open Prairies and the grandeur of the Rockies and the Arctic. The idea of this being damaged, through the practices of our own society or those of other countries, summons a profound response from us. It's something that we feel in our guts. It's something that says "No Way!"

Our reaction may also have to do with how we were brought up. Many of us grew up in small towns or on farms. We were able to wander around the countryside, go for hikes and picnics on Sundays, and swim where we wanted. We could fish in many small lakes and rivers. There was ready, unfettered access to a clean and seemingly inexhaustibly renewing environment.

Even those of us who grew up in cities still had a close connection to the land. Most of our cities were planned with abundant parks where children could play and explore. Many families had cottages, where they spent most of the summer. For others who did not have cottages, camping provided a less expensive means to travel around the country and enjoy the outdoors. Vacation areas with lakes and camping facilities were readily accessible.

Wherever we grew up in Canada, most of us had a sense of living in a vast, clean country with endless lakes, streams, forests and plains. We took it for granted. It was the only world we knew. Canadians did much less foreign traveling in those days, so we had fewer opportunities to compare our lifestyle with others'.

Of course, many Canadians were not born in Canada. Though they grew up in other countries, I suspect that they share much of this perception of Canada as vast and clean. In fact, their decision to immigrate to Canada may have been precipitated by an attraction to a country that seemed wide open, endless in size and opportunities.

The vastness of Canada in relation to the size of our population also leads to a special sense of connection to the land. This is more difficult to define than talking about summer camping holidays. It stretches back further in our history to when Europeans started coming to Canada to settle. The seemingly endlessness of the land was a constant amazement to the explorers and settlers.

Wave after wave of immigrants came. Culturally, we grew accustomed to thinking we had inexhaustible land available to cultivate. Of course, much of this land already was used by the native people. But that did not strike the new settlers as any reason to limit their aspirations. The sorry history of our disregard for the rights of Canada's native peoples continues today. Still, the fact remains that for generations it seemed that Canada had more land than could ever be filled with people.

Even today with our cities continuing to expand, even with most of the arable land cultivated and much of the accessible forest land used by the forest industry, a great deal of Canada's total land mass still remains as it has for centuries. In much of this land, in the northern parts of the provinces and in the northern territories, native people are the only ones in the area, continuing their ancient traditions of sustainable hunting, trapping and fishing.

We get some sense of the vastness of Canada when we fly over northern areas, or when we look at a map. I have a wall map of Canada in my office. Most of what I see, when I look at that map, is sparsely inhabited land. Way down at the bottom of the map, near the floor, is a narrow strip running along the U.S. border where almost all of us live.

Geographically, Canada could not support the population density of other countries, more of whose land is arable. Therefore, Canada has always had and always will have a relatively low population in relation to its size. This too contributed to our perception of this country. We conceive of ourselves as scattered people linked together largely by our land, our empty spaces.

This is one reason why I believe we have an untapped reservoir of resistance to the potential destruction of our

environment. Our identity as Canadians is too closely linked
to our physical conception of the land to be lost. We are
aware of the beauty of parts of the country that we have seen.
But we also carry with us, at a less conscious level, an appreciation of that vast area that few of us have experienced. Both
represent much of what this country means to us. Irreversible
environmental damage strikes not only at our love of the land
but also at our own identity as Canadians. We have identified
ourselves with the land. If it is threatened, so are we.

But we do not have to rely only on this mystical appreciation of Canada to ground our response to the environmental
crisis. It is coming more and more into our daily lives. The
media give us a steady stream of reasons to be worried about
our health and that of the children around us. We feel less and
less confident with the future we will leave to the next generation. We cry in our souls, "What is happening to this
earth?"

Distorting Christian theology

Many environmentalists have accused Christian theology
of contributing to the ecological crisis that we face. They
point to the references in Genesis of humanity being given
"dominion" over all creation. They contend that this has
provided the basis, ever since the industrial revolution, for
unfettered exploitation of the earth's resources with no
concern for environmental consequences. The earth was
created for humanity, we believed, and so we could do with it
as we wished in the name of the god "progress."

There may well be a relationship between the Christian
theological grounding of our western societies and the economic and industrial practices that developed over the past
150 years. We have seen ourselves as being the centre of the
universe. Everything in creation was for us to use as we
wished. Sometimes we saw nature as being neutral, so there
was no harm in our devastating it. Other times we saw it as
actually part of evil worldliness, as opposed to the goodness

of the spirit. That gave us even less compunction about doing with it as we wished. But this link of environmental problems and Christian theology is based on a distortion of the Bible that has been used to legitimize the expansionist aspirations of our societies.

A variety of theologians, for the past 15 years, have explored scripture to discern new ways of considering the relationship of humanity to the rest of creation. They concluded that God intended an *interdependent* relationship between humanity and the rest of creation, a relationship that requires *caring for* and *nurturing* of the earth.

Their insights can help to rectify the damage done by the earlier distortions of Christian theology. It can also give us some powerful new arguments for why we have no choice but to tackle the environmental threats to creation. Christian theology could move from being part of the problem to being a significant part of the solution.

Photo: Berkeley Studio

In exercising our dominion over creation without properly caring for it, we have misused our position as stewards of God's earth.

Our Faith
And the survival of creation

Many of you reading this book have a strong Christian faith. Many of you also are concerned about the environmental problems facing Canada and the world. But how much of a connection do you feel between those two commitments? I wanted to write this book because I saw that few of us Christians have any sense that caring about creation is an indispensable ingredient in our faith.

Some people believe that faith is primarily related to belief in God, in order to attain eternal life. They are likely to consider involvement in "social issues" a distraction for the Christian and for the church. Concern about the environment would fall low on their list of essentials for the Christian faith.

That rating of the importance of environmental problems would not differ much for many people who *do* believe that Christian faith requires them to be involved in social issues.

Fortunately, Canada has had a strong tradition of people who understood their faith as needing to be lived in concern about the poor, the disadvantaged and the oppressed. Through scripture and through the example of Christ's life and ministry, we feel called to be an expression of God's love for the suffering in the world. We demonstrate that commitment in many ways. Christians come to the aid of the neighboring farmer whose barn burned down. Congregations provide support for a refugee family. We write to our government on subjects like capital punishment and apartheid in South Africa. But the environment? We haven't seen it as an important concern for us as Christians.

Such faith is incomplete. Being unconcerned about creation represents a distortion of our biblical roots and an insensitivity to the presence of the Holy Spirit in our age. Both for the sake of our faith and for the survival of the environment, we have to make radical changes in our understanding of what it means to be Christian in relation to the rest of creation.

In this chapter, I look at our theology, to see how it may have contributed historically to the environmental crisis that we are in, how it may continue to give us some problems today, and what we can and must do to change our vision.

Religious roots of our attitudes toward nature

Distinctiveness of humans from the rest of creation

Are we as human beings an intrinsic part of creation or are we somehow distinct from it? The question has led to a great deal of confusion and controversy in Christian theology over the centuries. Understanding some of the roots of the controversy can perhaps help us deal with our present day theological difficulties when it comes to caring for the environment.

Christianity, and Judaism from which it grew, had a different approach to creation than did most of the other religions of ancient times. In the mythologies of some early civilizations, the earth was described either as the product of gods wanting servants to do their work for them or as the result of a sexual union of spirits with the female conceiving the creation. In both cases, human beings were very much part of that created order but of no higher value than the rest of it. The spirits of the gods were present not only in humans but in tools, animals, oceans, fire, stars and every element of nature.

These mythologies are full of battles between good spirits and evil spirits. Human beings were both pawns and active characters in these battles, as were other elements of nature. There was no significant distinction between humans and the rest.

The creation story in the Bible differs. It attributes to human beings a measure of distinctiveness from the rest of creation. God created Adam and Eve after the rest of nature and placed them in authority over it. Even more significantly, Adam and Eve were created in God's own image. God breathed directly into Adam the breath of life. It is interesting that in Hebrew, the word for breath is the same as the word for spirit. The story suggests that humans have a special kind of spiritual relationship to God, a closer, more intimate one than the rest of creation. It also implies that humans have a special relationship to the natural order, one of responsibility and authority. We call this type of elevation of the role of humanity in creation "anthropocentrism," literally "man-in-the-centre."

But this is not the whole story. The Genesis account describes human beings as being *part* of the creation. Within the context and progression of the creation of the earth, Adam and Eve were formed. They were placed in that creation and given nourishment from it. They are part of the ecological system. Adam was formed out of the dust of the ground. The biological nature of human beings is clearly there and never denied.

In the early days of the Christian church, theologians debated the true nature of humans and their relationship to the rest of creation. The side that won emphasized the spiritual component of humans and their distinctiveness within the created order.

This emphasis on the distinctiveness of human beings was reinforced by early interpretations of the nature of the rest of creation. Most other ancient civilizations believed that the spirits of the gods inhabited all the objects of the natural world. The Judeo-Christian tradition offered quite a different understanding. Nature was strictly physical. Nature was not itself divine. No aspect of creation other than humans had a spiritual quality.

Again we find only part of the picture being emphasized, as successive generations re-interpreted the Genesis account. Although nature may not be divine, God described it as being good. Many places in the Bible extol the wonder and beauty of creation. Yet, a strong current in Christian thought came to see all things material as evil.

The spiritual and the physical were regularly set against each other in the writings of theologians through the ages. To elevate the spiritual nature of humans, our physical side was put down. It was considered a source of evil.

This attitude toward the physical nature of *humans* was generalized to the *whole material world*. It is hard to raise much enthusiasm for caring about the natural order if one sees it as something to be subdued and suppressed. It is a logical next step, then, to argue that subduing and suppressing nature is a godly act, to be done by the higher order, the spiritual creatures of God—human beings.

Thus the predominant image that has been emphasized over the centuries: human beings are distinct from the rest of creation because they were created in God's image and were given authority over a natural order which, not being divine, is at least neutral and possibly negative. The fact that these images may not correspond to a fuller understanding of scripture has not historically lessened their power in influencing how western societies have related to the environment.

For the many centuries between the birth of Christianity and the industrial revolution, this religious attitude to creation had few serious consequences for the environment. The world's population was still relatively small. The economy was primarily agricultural. We did not yet have the technological power to affect the environment too dramatically. People struggled to survive; if anything, nature was viewed with respect—sometimes giving, and sometimes vindictive. The perspective of humanity as distinct from the rest of creation translated into little more than the need to learn how to live with nature.

Serious environmental problems began with the coming of the industrial revolution in the 1800s in Europe, and then in North America. Now the image of humans as distinct from the rest of creation took on new meaning. We learned how to use and transform more of the earth's resources for our own purposes. We started using coal to drive the engines of our industries and to heat our homes. We cut more and more lumber for the buildings of our cities. We expanded rapidly our knowledge of how to create new substances from minerals, biological material and other natural elements.

In the age of progress, Christian theology suited western societies just fine. God had endowed human beings with intelligence. Now these humans were fulfilling the divine plan by using that God-given intelligence to make new discoveries. The engineers of the new age saw the natural order as there for them to use for their own purposes. They firmly believed—at least at a subconscious level—that was why the world had been created. Humanity could do with nature what it wished.

Re-examining our "dominion" over all creation

Our theological heritage not only led us to believe that we were fundamentally different from the rest of creation, but also that we were fundamentally superior.

The Genesis version of creation reads in part: "And God said, 'Let us make man in our image, after our likeness: and let them have dominion over the fish of the sea, and over the fowl of the air, and over the cattle, and over all the earth, and over every creeping thing that creepeth on the earth.'" (Genesis 1:26)

This scripture sets forth a hierarchical order in creation. Man—literally man—is at the top. Woman, created after and from the man, comes next. Then all of the animals fall into line below them.

Psalm 8 uses even more graphic imagery:

What is man that thou art mindful of him?
And the son of man, that thou visitest him?
For thou *hast made him a little lower than the angels*,
And hast crowned him with glory and honor.

Thou *madest him to have dominion over the works of thy hands*
Thou *hast put all things under his feet:*
All sheep and oxen,
Yea, and the beasts of the field;
The fowl of the air, and the fish of the sea,
And whatsoever passeth through the paths of the seas.
(Psalm 8:3–8, KJV)

It is easy to understand how scriptures like these could lead to a belief in the superiority of humanity over the rest of creation. Western civilizations based on these religions

adopted this same perspective. They all saw the rest of the
created order as subservient to humans.

How are we to handle this dilemma? These scriptures
clearly appear to place humanity above nature, and to give
dominion over it. On the other hand, this same sense of
ownership of and authority over nature has done much to
erase human respect for the rest of creation. We have exploited and polluted it at will.

We do not have the option to rewrite those scriptures.
Should we try to re-interpret them, or pay less attention to
some points as unhelpful and even destructive? I think that
we have to do some of both.

The context for the Genesis reference to "dominion" is
usually forgotten. The reference to humanity being given
dominion comes right after God deciding to create us in
God's own image. God assigned the authority of dominion
while man and woman were still assumed to function as God
would. And God, we must remember, created the world, and
all that was in it, and called it "good."

Later, sin entered the picture. Adam and Eve were not
satisfied with being humans made in the image of God. They
yielded to the temptation to be gods themselves. They were
tempted to eat of the forbidden tree of knowledge of good and
evil, so that "your eyes shall be opened, and ye shall be as
gods" (Genesis 3:5). God had explicitly told them not to eat
the fruit of that tree. They disobeyed.

I find an interesting parallel, that their sin was greed and
lust for power to be like a god. These same characteristics
have caused our present problems with our environment. Our
societies have treated nature as if it were their personal
property. We have seen ourselves as powerful gods who can
subdue creation, and who have the authority to do so. God
intended humanity to be *in the image of God* not to try and be
a god itself.

Perhaps if these sins of greed and power-seeking had not
entered the scene, humanity might have been able to exercise

"dominion" in a more appropriate way, caring for the created order as God would. But such has not been the case.

So what can we do about the dominion symbolism in the Bible? I think that we have to admit that our sinfulness has blinded us, and that we have misunderstood. Then we have to leave this distorted understanding behind us. The concept of dominion is part of our history, but we can no longer accept it. We must reject it as contrary to the broader intention of God. Unless we reject the dominion theme, our societies run the risk of continuing to destroy not only much of nature but human life as well.

Some of the most helpful writings in recent years on these questions have come from feminist theologians. They found similarities between the ways certain scriptural references have caused difficulties in male/female relationships, and the ways those same passages contributed to a destructive attitude toward nature. The underlying problem—in both relationships—has to do with the seeking for power and control.

It is always hard to think that parts of the Bible are no longer helpful. We fear being accused of denying the authority of scripture. We worry about where we should draw the line about what parts of the Bible we discard, and what parts remain still pivotal to our faith. There are no easy answers.

We can try to understand the scriptures in the historical context in which they were written. But mainly we have to trust the presence of God's spirit in our lives, to help us discern the will and direction of God in our day. We will always gain much guidance from the Bible. But God also acts in our present world. God today calls us to repentance for abusing creation, in the name of having dominion over it. God calls us to change our ways.

Giving some value to this world

A powerful tradition throughout our history claims that this world is unimportant. It is only a transitional phase that we have to pass through in order to reach the next life.

Here lies one of the biggest theological stumbling blocks to a Christian concern for the environment. It is another example of a Christian doctrine taken to an extreme, and then used as an excuse to avoid caring about God's creation.

We believe in an afterlife. We take the scriptures seriously when they talk about God sending Jesus so that we might be saved and have everlasting life. When we die, we believe our earthly body ceases to function; our soul lives on. We do not know what that next life will be like, and most of us feel uncomfortable talking about it very much. But we believe in it. We recognize that this belief distinguishes our Christian faith from the atheism of much of our society.

So far so good. But problems for the environment start to develop when we draw implications for this world from our belief in the next. Those implications range from apathy to open antagonism. In terms of apathy, if this life is merely an interlude before we become united with God, then it doesn't really matter what happens to the earth. This world is of no particular importance. Environmental problems come to be seen as little more than nuisances which make present life somewhat less comfortable. But there certainly is no reason, according to this view, for us to spend our time and energy doing something about these problems.

This attitude sometimes takes a stronger form. If we need to be "saved" from this world in order to get to the next, then some suggest that this world is not just unimportant or neutral, but actually evil. They contrast the physical, material nature of this world with the spiritual nature of the next. If that spiritual next life is by definition good, then this earthly existence must be bad.

This kind of attitude does not often surface consciously. Indeed humans give more evidence of actively *pursuing* the material life than of trying to avoid it. People want more and more. The desire for ever more consumer goods, the demand for ever increasing energy to feed all our machines are signs not of abandoning the physical world but of lusting for it.

But this is still not a relationship of caring and respect for creation. It sees the earth as just there to meet our voracious appetites. The consequences end up pretty much the same as saying that the physical world is evil. Either way, creation is not viewed as having any spiritual value. We are not drawn to care for it, to respect it. Our exploitative and polluting ways go on unchallenged.

Pursuing a theology that loves the creation

For most of the history of Christianity, theology has not expressed much concern about the earth. As I have suggested, certain themes arising out of scripture have been exaggerated out of context to support a disregard or even hatred for the elements of this world. Those theological distortions have contributed to a mindset in our western societies which has sanctioned the exploitation and polluting of the earth in the interests of so-called human progress.

Many of our hymns reflect the ways we see the world around us. Most of the time, the earth is ignored. They make no connection between how we live and the well-being of the planet. Sometimes we sing highly romanticized hymns, with God and nature all tied up together. These imply that we need not worry. Creation is beautiful. God will protect it. But God has not made that promise.

The environmental problems facing us today are so serious that unless we tackle them head on, our earth will be irrevocably changed. All forms of life will be threatened. For God's sake, for this earth's sake, for our sake, can't we wake up?

We who are Christian can and must play a major role in turning the tide. The same strands of Christian theology which have been wedded so closely to our economic and political development now threaten creation. Of course, we should not overestimate the impact of theological concepts on the direction of our culture over the past few centuries. But neither can we in conscience deny that they have played a significant role in forming the value base which legitimized the exploitation of the earth for the purposes of progress.

I believe that we owe something to our societies to make up for this history. We certainly have a responsibility to other parts of the world whose cultures have not yet been influenced by these theological justifications for disregarding the earth, but who still have to share the consequences with us. They may be creating environmental problems of their own. But we need to be careful about trying to remove the speck in their eye while the log still juts from ours.

Ultimately, we have a much more important reason for our involvement in protecting creation than guilty feelings about past errors. Our scriptures and theological tradition contain the seeds for a radically different understanding of the role of human beings in relation to the rest of creation. If nurtured, these seeds could grow to have a profound influence on the future of the planet. I believe that we can provide theological insights, a vision, that could lead to a much greater valuing of this earth and all that is in it. From being part of the problem, we could become a powerful part of the solution.

This will present major challenges to the faith that we have grown used to. Certain aspects will have to receive much more emphasis; others may need to be abandoned. But our faith will be richer for it. Further, our faith will finally have some relevance to our concern about the future of creation. The pervasive, gnawing anxiety shared by many Canadians about threats to the environment will find a strong basis in Christian values. The need to do something about these threats will become a Christian imperative.

God loves creation

In the creation story of the Jewish and Christian faiths, God forms the earth out of chaos. Step by step, each element came into being. First there was light, and day and night existed. Then the earth emerged as separate from the heavens and the seas, with dry land. God filled the earth with vegetation, the seas with fish, the land with animals. God placed stars, sun and moon in the sky. Finally, God created man and woman. "And God saw everything that he had made, and behold, it was very good." (Genesis 1:31, RSV)

As Christians, we believe that God did create the world. Most of us do not assume that it was done as literally as Genesis describes it. We have learned through science of the origins of the earth and the process of evolution. (Science portrays no less a miracle of creation than the story in Genesis.) The natural world inspires our admiration—the beauty of a flower, the awesomeness of space, the wonder of the human body. We acknowledge God as the creator of it all, a mysterious power beyond our comprehension.

But a force even greater than *power* was responsible for creation. Love. God created the earth and human beings as part of it, out of *love*. God sought a *relationship*. All creation was interrelated—the skies with the earth, the plants with the animals, man and woman with the rest of creation. And God was related to it *all*. And God was pleased with it.

We know the joy we feel when we produce something truly wonderful. The creating of new human life, through the miracle of conception and birth, is probably the ultimate such experience. The love which bonds parents and children has its genesis in that act of creation. How much greater must be the love that God experiences at being the creator not only of one human being but of life itself?

God's love for creation flows through scripture. The forgiving love of God is constantly demonstrated through the history of the Israelite people in the Old Testament. The ultimate expression of that love is the sending of God's own child to redeem the creation that is in such trouble. *"For God so loved the world, that he gave his only Son . . . not to condemn the world, but that the world might be saved through him."* (John 3:16–17, RSV)

Nothing in the Genesis story, or subsequently in the Old or New Testament, indicates that God felt anything but a deep love for creation. God is depicted as constantly involved in creating and sustaining creation through God's "word," "wisdom," "spirit," "name," and "hand." God loves creation. Profoundly. All of it.

We are called to be stewards of God's creation

An image in the Bible of the relationship of human beings to the rest of creation deserves a lot more attention than it has received—the image of steward. It offers us a vision of how we can relate to the rest of creation in a way that will protect and care for it rather than conquering and exploiting it as we have done and continue to do. (Note the books of Douglas John Hall on this theme.)

Both the Old and the New Testaments describe the role of the steward. The Old Testament gives technical descriptions of the position and responsibilities of the steward within the household. The New Testament uses these as the basis for a more general image of stewardship.

The office of steward as depicted in the Old Testament has a number of important characteristics. The steward is very important in the household, occupying a position of some authority. The role differs from that of other servants. The steward is more like a supervisor in charge of the household, and has a very close relationship to the owner. The steward is taken into the confidence of the master, and is seen as an official representative of the master.

Despite this important position in the household, the steward is still a servant and not a master. The steward exercises authority only as granted by the master. The steward is responsible to the master. The household personnel, belongings and activities over which the steward exercises authority all belong to the master. The steward who fails to execute responsibilities appropriately can and will be punished, or replaced. Isaiah 22 describes the harsh punishment awaiting any steward who becomes too arrogant and assumes the role of the master.

These characteristics are developed in the New Testament references. In his parables, Jesus assumes the role of master; those who would follow Jesus are placed in the role of the steward. The various parables make clear that these stewards/ followers will be held accountable for how they exercise their responsibility. That accountability shows most forcefully in Luke 12, where the senior servant or steward abuses the household over which he has responsibility. The steward is punished and thrown out.

I see strong parallels between these pictures of the steward in a household and our relationship with creation. We are part of creation and have some responsibility for it. But like the steward, we do not own the property. "The earth is the Lord's and the fullness thereof; the world and they that dwell therein," Psalm 24:1 reminds us. To assume that we own the earth, its resources, or its inhabitants, is distinctly unbiblical.

The steward image helps us to resolve some troubling aspects of our relationship to the rest of creation. On the one hand, it does acknowledge that human beings have a special relationship to God and to the rest of creation. This special relationship reflects both the creation story and our own experience. It suggests that the master has chosen us for some special role in the household/world. Human beings *do* occupy a different position than other elements of creation.

Yet that role is one of caretaker and gardener. We are not the owners, entitled to do as we wish. As stewards of God's property, our role is to care for it *as the master would*. We are the master's representatives. Therefore, we need to act toward that for which we have responsibility in the same way the master would.

By contrast, we have traditionally looked on the earth and its resources as belonging to *us* to do with as *we* will. We have used it with no other criteria than meeting our own needs and desires.

Even more troubling than our exploitation of the earth's resources has been our disregard for the environmental consequences of our human activity. We have treated God's earth as a massive garbage dump. Instead of lovingly caring for that over which we have been given some responsibility, we have recklessly abused it. If we take seriously our role as stewards, we can no longer maintain that view.

God will hold us accountable for what happens to the earth. The destructive effect of our pollution is not simply an inconvenience for us, or even an unfortunate legacy for future generations. We are destroying what belongs to God.

Learning to live *with* the rest of creation

God created the earth and loves it. As part of that creation, we have been given some particular responsibilities for it. We are to exercise those responsibilities as obedient stewards. Our role is to care for the earth, recognizing that it belongs not to us but to God.

Therefore, we have to give up relating to the earth as if we could do with it as we wished. We have to find a new way of relating to the earth. We have to learn to live *with* the rest of creation.

Learning to live with the rest of creation will require a level of humility that has not been very evident in recent human history. This humility starts with accepting that we do not own the earth; it is God's. We are not even *renting* it. We are here because God *chose to include us in creation*. We are on earth by the grace of God.

We should be considerably humbled simply from recognizing how dependent we are upon the rest of creation for our survival. We need air to breathe; we need food from the land and the sea for nourishment. The reverse is not equally true. The earth could get along very well without us. It does not depend on human beings for its existence.

When we realize this, the way we have misused the earth appears not only incredibly arrogant but also terribly short-sighted and self-destructive.

To learn to live *with* the rest of creation will require developing a better understanding of our place within it. We have for too long emphasized our distinctiveness from other elements of nature. We now need to focus on how we are similar to the rest of creation and how we can fit into it.

This is where the scientific concept of "ecosystem" has theological relevance. "Ecosystem" is a relatively new term, referring to the way all living organisms interact with each other. The concept helps illustrate the interdependence of all life. What affects one will have repercussions for all. The health of the environment as a whole is critical to the survival of all its parts.

We are part of this earthly ecosystem. As biological creatures, we depend on other parts of our environment for survival. At the same time, what we do affects other elements in the ecosystem. Our theology needs to take very seriously this lesson from biology. God created us out of the same physical elements as the rest of nature, and placed us within this garden paradise called earth. We must learn how to live in it as one element of the whole created order.

To live compatibly with the rest of creation, we need to better understand how it works. Human intelligence is one of the wonders of God's creation. It can delve deep into the mysteries of God's universe. Much that we have learned through medical research has dramatically improved the lives of humans around the world. But scientific research has also been exploited. It has been used to further human domination of the created order, to create more and more to feed our insatiable consumer appetites, to make bigger arms to destroy others. We desperately need to direct human intelligence towards a better understanding of the physical, biological and chemical functioning of the earth. Now more than ever we need to know what we can and cannot do to live in harmony with all of creation.

There is no question that we have the capacity to learn much more than we presently know. But our intelligence implies greater responsibility not greater privilege. "To whom much is given, of him will much be required" (Luke 12:48, RSV). Other elements in nature already exist in compatibility with each other. They have neither the need nor capacity to understand how that relationship functions. Human beings are the creatures who have not been coexisting in a healthy way with the rest. But we can learn how.

Research to understand the mysteries of this world will require many bright young minds. We need young people willing to dedicate their lives to generating the knowledge that will help us change our ways. That is asking a lot. Previous generations have been responsible for setting the world on this present destructive course. The same generations enjoyed unprecedented material and lifestyle benefits. But the environmental costs of that progress are only now becoming apparent. Future generations will have to pay for those benefits.

Perhaps it is presumptuous of those who benefitted to ask those who will pay the price to assist us in learning better how the world functions. But we have no choice. We can only pray that they will be wiser and more future-oriented than we have been. And we can only hope that they can forgive those of us who have gone before.

In the need to understand this world better, in order to know how to fit into it, we must be careful not to over-emphasize the potential of human intelligence. Intelligence and vanity are closely related. We will never know *everything* about the mysteries of this created order. We must never let an increasing level of knowledge tempt us back into the arrogance that characterized our relationship with the rest of creation so far. Our pursuit of a better understanding of this world must be to develop a more compatible coexistence of humanity within it.

This is one of the risks in the concept of stewardship. We can easily slide from caring for creation to feeling that we know best. Stewardship requires a constant sense of humility and accountability.

Working together for eco-justice

Learning to live in a compatible relationship with the rest
of creation has implications for our relationship with each
other. We are called to live in a right relationship not only
with other species on the planet, but with our own as well.

Some approaches to environmental protection, by both
advocates and detractors, have set environmental concerns
against the economic well-being of workers. The argument
gets put most simply as jobs versus the environment. This is a
false dichotomy. An approach that emphasizes the long-term
health of the earth ought also to underline the importance of
an equitable sharing of resources and opportunities for all
people.

This is what is meant by the new term "eco-justice." The
word may be new, but the concept is not. The Old Testament
saw justice in the social order closely linked to the health and
integrity of creation. "The Lord upholds all who are falling
down, and raises up all who are bowed down. The eyes of all
look to you, and you give them their food in due season. You
open your hand, and satisfy the desire of every living thing,"
says Psalm 145:14–16 (RSV). Pursuit of a sustainable lifestyle does not automatically lead to social justice. But the two
are compatible. Justice must always be present as we seek to
safeguard the integrity of creation, and vice versa.

This can work in practical ways in the decisions we make.
For instance, we currently use non-renewable energy sources
like coal, oil and gas at an alarming rate. The plants that burn
these fossil fuels are also a major source of pollution contributing to acid rain, the global warming trend and the depletion
of the ozone layer. They are increasingly capital-intensive industries; that is, they rely on large complex technology rather
than a lot of jobs.

There is an alternative. Some Canadian researchers have
documented how Canada could place much greater emphasis
on energy conservation, and on developing renewable energy
sources. This would sustain, for a longer period, our non-

renewable energy sources and reduce environmental pollution. The strategy of conservation and renewable energy would also produce many more long-term jobs than do our present megaprojects and big electrical generating stations. In other words, job creation and the preservation of the environment are compatible.

A sustainable lifestyle will not solve all of our problems. There will inevitably be conflicts. Working at social justice and ecological health will create its own share of tensions. But the alternative is to continue our present destructive practices. Churches can play a helpful role in providing an opportunity for these tensions to be discussed and dealt with constructively.

Our Christian theology has been used over the years to justify the plundering of the earth's resources and the neglecting of the consequences of our pollution. We can turn that around. Within the Bible and our theology lie powerful arguments for defining a new, just and loving relationship between humanity and the rest of creation.

As Christians, we can make a positive difference to the future of creation. We can learn to care for the earth. We must.

Resources for further information

Christian Ecology, Building an Environmental Ethic for the Twenty-First Century, Ed. Fred Krueger, (Apr. 1988), The North American Conference on Christianity and Ecology, P.O. Box 14305, San Francisco, CA, 94114

The Earth is the Lord's—Essays on Stewardship, Edited by Mary Evelyn Jegen and Bruno V. Manno, Paulist Press, NY, 1978.

Ecology and Religion—Toward a New Christian Theology of Nature, John Carmody, Paulist Press, NY, 1983

For Creation's Sake—Preaching, Ecology and Justice, Edited by Dieter T. Hessel, The Geneva Press, Philadelphia, 1985

Green Paradise Lost, Elizabeth Dobson Gray, Roundtable Press, Wellesley, 1981

The Steward—A Biblical Symbol Come of Age, Douglas John Hall, Friendship Press, NY, 1982

Thomas Berry and the New Cosmology, edited by Anne Lonergan and Caroline Richards, Twenty-Third Publications, Mystic, 1987

To Work and To Love—a Theology of Creation, Dorothee Soelle with Shirley A. Cloyes, Fortress Press, Philadelphia, 1984

Materials from the *World Council of Churches* on *Justice, Peace and the Integrity of Creation*, 150 rue de Ferney, 1121 Geneva 20, Switzerland

Photo courtesy of INCO

*INCO's superstack at their Sudbury refinery has become an
international symbol of acid rain.*

Acid Rain
Poison from the sky

Acid rain in Canada is a frightening story. Acid rain causes
devastating damage to our lakes, rivers, fish, ducks, trees, and
to our own health, and it increases year by year. But the acid
rain story also contains a germ of hope for the future. More
than any other environmental issue, it has united Canadians,
particularly those in Central Canada. No one argues against
stopping acid rain. We all are frightened of the impact that it
has and are determined to do something about it.

Canadian newspapers are regularly filled with stories about
acid rain. A recent article indicated that acid rain damage to

sugar maples in Quebec is much more serious than was previously thought. An area of Quebec formerly assumed to be free of acid rain problems now shows half its maple trees losing much of their foliage. This loss of leaves is an early indicator of serious acid rain damage. Quebec used to be called the maple syrup capital of the world; the days of that reputation may be numbered. Quebec's 8,000 maple syrup producers estimate that they have lost up to $110 million income because of acid rain.

It is sadly appropriate that the maple tree should be so vulnerable to acid rain. The maple leaf is the official symbol of Canada. It represents this land. If the maple dies, so does part of the essence of Canada.

Everybody knows what acid rain is. Polls indicate that almost all Canadians, and many Americans, know about this menace to the environment. Yet as recently as the mid-1970s, the term "acid rain" was virtually unknown.

Awareness of the problem has grown rapidly. The media regularly report research detailing how many lakes are being killed, and how trees are dying. Now new evidence links human respiratory problems to acid rain. The highly political nature of acid rain, as a major conflict between Canada and the U.S., also makes it a big media story.

What acid rain does to our environment

Like many other things that seem unfair in life, acid rain hurts the most vulnerable and defenseless parts of nature first. Because of prevailing wind patterns, clouds full of sulphur dioxide and nitrogen oxides from central Canada and the U.S. drift northeast over the most susceptible areas of the continent, where the soils are thinnest and the bedrock is granite. These areas have little natural limestone to counteract the acidity falling in the rain.

"Clean rain" has a pH count of 5.6 (the pH scale is a chemist's term to refer to the acidity or alkalinity of a solution). When acid rain increases acidity of lakes and rivers, the pH count goes down. At a pH level of 5.0, many fish species no longer reproduce; frogs and salamanders cannot survive. If a water system reaches a pH of 4.5, all fish life will be dead.

In a recent Ontario study of 4000 lakes, 155 were almost completely dead; nearly 3000 showed serious acidification. A dozen rivers in Nova Scotia can no longer support Atlantic salmon. U.S. research suggests that over half of the lakes in the eastern states receive sufficient acid rain to have significant damage.

To compound the problem, these geologically sensitive areas also get a lot of snow. Sulphur dioxide and nitrogen oxides fall in snow just as in rain. But in snow they do not enter water systems immediately. Rather, the acids are stored in the accumulating snow. Then in spring, just as most fish and amphibians enter their spawning or reproductive periods, melting snow releases the pollutants into the streams and lakes all at once. The massive onslaught is referred to as acid shock. Water from melting snow has been found to be up to 100 times more acidic than normal.

When acid rain falls on land, it gradually sinks in and makes its way underground. There it can dissolve metals in the earth like aluminum, mercury, cadmium and lead. The levels of these poisonous metals become much higher than normal in water systems. Increased levels of aluminum clog the gills of fish, causing them to suffocate and die. Aluminum has also been linked to Alzheimer's disease in humans. Other metals that accumulate in fish tissue harm the birds, animals and people who eat them.

Larger animals that live around water systems—ducks, loons, herons, otter and mink—suffer from eating fish and other aquatic life. They also gradually run out of food as the lakes and rivers become too acidified to support life.

Not only water systems, and those creatures that live in and around them, are affected by acid rain. Increasing evidence shows that forests are starting to be hit too. Sugar maples in

Quebec are dying at an alarming rate. Beech, red maple and yellow birch in New Brunswick and Nova Scotia also show signs of decline.

Acid rain apparently interferes with photosynthesis in the leaves of some trees. It increases the vulnerability of trees to disease and insects. Higher levels of acidity affect decomposition on the forest floor, altering the natural cycle of growth and decay which replenishes the soil feeding the trees.

Scientists now expect serious damage to Canada's forests in the future, as trees lose their abilities to survive the effects of acid rain. The forest industry in Canada employs a million people directly and indirectly, almost one out of every ten jobs in this country. No other industry contributes as much to Canada's balance of payments, with $13 billion in exports annually. We are in for some devastating economic impacts if predictions of forest destruction from acid rain come true.

Acid rain also affects other parts of our society. Agriculture may be hurt in some areas. In our cities, buildings are getting eaten away and requiring increasingly frequent repairs—estimated at billions of dollars annually before long.

Human health is the main question mark right now. Some initial research correlates heavy acid precipitation with significant increases at hospitals of people having respiratory problems. Maybe only damage to our own health will convince us that the costs of acid rain have become too high.

Where acid rain comes from

Our industrial/consumer lifestyle is very costly ecologically. Acid rain is one of those costs.

Large ore smelters spew out tonnes of sulphur dioxide and nitrogen oxides from their smokestacks. Coal-burning power plants pump out massive quantities of these same emissions. Oil refineries and other industrial facilities contribute a smaller share. The cars and trucks that we drive emit nitrogen oxides into the atmosphere.

These invisible gases drift through the atmosphere. There, they are transformed by sunlight and moisture into sulphuric acid and nitric acid. As the water vapor falls to earth in the form of rain or snow, it carries with it this deadly cargo of dissolved acids. By the time these chemicals reach earth as acid rain, the pollutants may have travelled hundreds or thousands of kilometres from their sources.

Though debates continue about how much damage acid rain causes, no one disputes where the pollution originates. Most of the Canadian sulphur dioxide comes from the huge INCO smelter at Sudbury, Ontario, and the Noranda smelter in northwest Quebec. Most American acid rain comes from coal-burning power plants in the Ohio Valley.

INCO comes around—slowly

INCO's superstack at their Sudbury refinery has become an international symbol of acid rain. Ironically, it was built to combat air pollution. The Sudbury area had suffered for years because of pollution from INCO's smelter. The world's largest chimney was intended to disperse the emissions beyond Sudbury. In fact, the air quality around Sudbury did improve significantly after the stack was completed in 1972. But though the tonnes of sulphur being emitted from the stack no longer fell on Sudbury, they hadn't disappeared. Rather they dispersed over a wider area, remaining in the atmosphere longer, allowing more of the chemicals to be changed by water vapor into sulphuric acid and to fall as acid rain.

Sulphur dioxide has been released by INCO (and its predecessors) in the Sudbury area since 1886. By 1916, 600,000 tonnes of sulphur dioxide were being emitted each year, with an average *daily* output of 1644 tonnes. Over the decades, the Sudbury smelter became one of the major international sources of nickel. But the price being paid for that prosperity was a staggering amount of pollution. By 1960, INCO spewed on average 6,218 tonnes of sulphur dioxide into the atmosphere *every day of the year!*

As a society, we were slow to recognize the disastrous effects of these emissions. The poor quality of Sudbury's air was the most obvious problem. That was tackled by building progressively taller smokestacks, to send the offending emissions farther and farther afield. Both INCO and the rest of us seemed to assume that if the pollution was sent high enough it would disappear and cause no problem.

For decades, this plume of destructive fumes continued unchallenged. The provincial government in Ontario did start responding to public concern in the late '60s. They ordered INCO to reduce its emissions from 5,000 tonnes per day to 750 by 1978. When the deadline arrived, however, INCO was still emitting over 3,600 tonnes per day. They claimed that they could do no better. The government accepted their arguments. INCO claimed to have no money for pollution control. Yet at the same time they spent a reported $238 million in 1974 buying the largest battery manufacturer in the U.S. as an investment. Protecting the environment has, for most of our history, been viewed as a luxury, not a necessity. In this case, clearly, the environment came well below profit motives.

In 1980, public pressure pushed the government to start leaning on INCO again. The province ordered INCO to reduce emissions to 2500 tonnes per day immediately, and to 1950 tonnes per day by mid-1983. In September of 1983, representatives of the churches met with senior INCO management. Company officials frankly admitted that INCO pollution was a major contributor to continental acid rain, but argued that their financial situation prevented them from doing anything more in the immediate future.

Arguments between INCO, groups concerned about the environment, and the government continued. Eventually the company announced it would reduce its emissions by the year 1994 to under 1,000 tonnes per day. The Government of Ontario has imposed strict regulations to ensure that INCO makes these reductions. Though federal and provincial money was available, INCO decided to pay for the clean-up of their emissions themselves. It will cost about $500 million!

INCO continues to be the largest single-point source of sulphur dioxide emissions in North America. But cutting their emissions to the 1994 target would represent a 70% reduction from 1980 levels. This would make a significant contribution to Canada's goal of reducing 1980 levels by 50% by 1994.

Noranda demands tax dollars to clean up

Noranda contrasts strikingly in corporate attitude with INCO. For years, the official position of Noranda was that what goes up doesn't necessarily come down. They acknowledged that their Horne Smelter at Rouyn-Noranda in northwest Quebec emitted a lot of sulphur dioxide. But they also steadfastly maintained that they were not a significant contributor to acid rain.

Noranda began smelting ore from a large copper mine in the area in 1923. Eventually, that ore body was exhausted. The smelter now handles ore transported from distant mines. The local environment around the smelter was devastated over the years by the sulphur emissions. Luc Chartrand, writing in *Quebec Science*, described the area as "an open wound in the northwestern ecosystem: dead lakes, defoliated forests where even the humus has disappeared."

As at INCO, the initial strategy to deal with local air pollution was to build smoke stacks that would send the emissions farther afield. Two stacks 160 and 140 metres high successfully decreased the sulphur dioxide emissions that fell in the immediate vicinity, by sending them greater distances.

The Horne Smelter is now the second largest single source of sulphur dioxide emissions in North America. In 1965, it spewed out 704,000 tonnes of sulphur dioxide. For most of the '70s, annual emission levels ranged between 514,000 to 608,000. In 1982, it still discharged about 555,000 tonnes.

Noranda has frequently added an emotionally powerful argument to avoid emission control programs. The company has threatened to close the plant if they are forced to pay for

new pollution control technologies. The Horne Smelter is old.
Modernizing to reduce emissions would be expensive. And
since the ore that the smelter handles has to be transported
into the area anyway, there may be valid reasons for question-
ing the continuation of the operation at all. But it is one of the
few sources of employment in an economically depressed
area—so the threat has plenty of clout.

Nevertheless, the Horne Smelter produced profits of
millions of dollars annually for Noranda for decades. And
despite their threats, the company shows no plans to close it
in the immediate future.

Finally, the provincial government of Quebec decided to
get tough. In July 1984, they announced plans to force Noranda to reduce sulphur dioxide emissions from the Horne
Smelter by 50% by 1989. Simultaneously, the Quebec Ministry of the Environment released a study documenting Noranda's contribution to the acid rain problem in the province.

Complex negotiations on cost-sharing occupied the next
couple of years. In early 1987, Noranda, and the federal and
provincial governments agreed to share the costs of construct-
ing a facility at Noranda to transform sulphur dioxide into
sulphuric acid. Acid rain-causing emissions would be reduced
by 45%.

Canada's second largest contributor to acid rain was also
being brought into line—with hefty incentives of fines and of
tax dollars to aid their modernization! Canada's goal of reducing its emissions that create acid rain by 50% had taken
another major step forward.

With Noranda, the offer of public funds was necessary to
get the company to adopt major pollution reduction programs.
This raises a significant question of social ethics. Is it appropriate for the public to have to contribute to the clean-up costs
for a private company? Or should the one profiting from the
pollution bear the expense? A political decision was made, to
be willing to spend tax dollars, because of the seriousness of
the problem and the likelihood that it would not be dealt with

without financial assistance. Public opinion polls show support for those decisions. But was it right?

Ontario Hydro embarrasses Canadians

Ontario Hydro represents a different set of problems. Here a publicly-owned utility is one of the major Canadian contributors to acid rain. With such anger among Canadians about acid rain, I consider it something of a scandal that a public corporation should be so negligent in controlling emissions. The Parliamentary Sub-committee on Acid Rain did not mince words in their 1983 report *Time Lost*:

> This Crown Corporation, the largest and most powerful utility in the country, situated in Canada's industrial heartland, has the responsibility to lead the way in acid rain control, to set an example for other industries to emulate. That it has not done so, but instead has forfeited its leadership role, is at best unworthy and, at worst, irresponsible. (p. 23)

Ontario Hydro's sources of sulphur dioxide and nitrogen oxide emissions are primarily their coal-burning electrical generating plants. Hydro operates five coal-burning power plants. In 1980, these facilities released about 452,000 tonnes. This represents about 20% of all sulphur dioxide emissions in Ontario that year.

Hydro has constantly shifted their response to criticism about acid rain. At certain times, they have suggested converting the plants from coal to gas. At other times, they have claimed that because demand for electricity was falling, they would need to use the coal-fired plants less, thus reducing emissions anyway. Using lower sulphur coal from Alberta could also produce fewer emissions than the high sulphur coal that Hydro imported from the U.S. But their major argument has been that if they build more nuclear plants, their dependence upon the coal will diminish. For those of us who do not view nuclear power with particular enthusiasm, this strategy leaves much to be desired.

None of these approaches has been successful. Only one Toronto generating facility was converted to gas. Recently, Hydro has revised upwards their projections for electricity demand. They also claim that they cannot afford lower sulphur coal from Alberta. They say that U.S. high sulphur coal is cheaper for them. Recurring problems with the nuclear plants, that have required some extensive and expensive shutdowns for repair, resulted in even more use of coal-burning stations, and thus even higher emissions.

Ontario Hydro has always tried to avoid the most effective strategy of all for reducing emissions from coal-burning plants. Devices called scrubbers can reduce sulphur dioxide emissions by up to 90%. The process simply involves spraying limestone into the furnace, where it mixes with the sulphur dioxide, trapping it in a solid sediment.

Hydro estimates the cost of installing scrubbers at about $500 million per plant. As part of their on-again, off-again campaign against installing scrubbers, Hydro has sometimes tried to scare consumers by suggesting how much this expense would add to their hydro bills. That approach has not generated much sympathy for Ontario Hydro. Public concern about acid rain is sufficiently high that people do not seem to mind the prospect of paying a bit more a month if it will help.

Another strategy that could make a big difference—if Ontario Hydro were to accept it as a central part of their mandate—is encouraging Ontario residents and industry to conserve energy. We have a vast potential for energy conservation in Canada. We have been slow to recognize that producing more and more energy causes major environmental problems. Acid rain is only one of these problems. Coal-burning plants also release a lot of carbon dioxide, which contributes to the global warming trend. Unfortunately, Ontario Hydro still seems to want to continuously expand their production capacity. Their gestures toward energy conservation pale in comparison to their expansion activities.

Ontario governments have often appeared weak-kneed towards Ontario Hydro, as if the utility were an empire unto itself, answerable to no one. The historic willingness of the government to accept Hydro's excuses for not reducing their acid rain causing emissions lends credence to that criticism.

But the Ontario government has gradually gotten tougher with Hydro. In 1981, they ordered Hydro to reduce its sulphur dioxide emission by 43% by 1990. That would bring their emissions down to 260,000 tonnes annually. Four years later in 1985, new regulations were adopted to force Ontario Hydro to reduce emissions of sulphur dioxide to 175,000 tonnes by 1994. Hydro may finally have to install scrubbers or some other equally effective pollution control device on their coal-burning plants. The image of a public corporation having to be pushed into acting in a socially responsible way has embarrassed Canadians, particularly Ontario residents.

Ontario Hydro's behavior has certainly not helped Canada's case in arguing for acid rain controls south of the border. Though the U.S. has many more coal-fired power plants than we do, at least some have installed scrubbers. Canadians trying to put pressure on the U.S. have always felt particularly vulnerable, lest Ontario Hydro's record be used to undermine our position. What makes it so galling is that such embarrassment should be caused by a *public* utility. (In dealing with corporations, the churches have found that public corporations are not necessarily more sensitive to the public mood than are private ones.)

Transportation receives tougher control standards

As well as sulphur dioxide, coal-burning electrical plants and smelters also emit some nitrogen oxides, but in much smaller quantities. We, the general public, create most of the nitrogen oxides that contribute to acid rain. They come from transportation, and about a third of the total is produced by our cars.

Emissions from our cars contribute largely to acid rain. Even with tough emission control standards, must there be so many cars?

For years, Canada lagged far behind the United States in standards for auto emissions. Until the mid-1980s, Canada allowed emissions of 3.1 grams of nitrogen oxides per vehicle-mile, more than three times the U.S. standard of 1.0. (California had an even more restricted limit of 0.4.) In the early stages of our battle with the Americans over acid rain, this undercut our credibility as much as Ontario Hydro did.

The Canadian Coalition on Acid Rain and other concerned groups, including some of the churches in Canada, pressed the federal government for years to make auto standards more stringent. The government's slowness to move was always a mystery to us. Granted, a strong lobby from the petroleum industry and the car makers wanted to leave standards as they were. But the arguments of these two groups seemed weak since tougher standards were already in place in the U.S.

Ironically—perhaps pathetically—the lobby group of the petroleum industry fighting those stricter standards was called PACE, the Petroleum Association for Conservation of the Canadian Environment!

In any case, concern about the contribution of nitrogen oxides to acid rain eventually prevailed. The federal government announced in 1985 that new cars and light trucks in

Canada would be forced to meet tougher control standards, effective September 1987.

The United States resists action

Here, the going gets tough. Dealing with the United States has never been easy for Canadians. For most of our history, we have coexisted as friendly neighbors. But when conflicts arise, the drastic difference in population size puts Canadians at a considerable disadvantage.

For over a decade acid rain has been one of those conflicts. The American reaction to growing awareness of acid rain has varied from complacency to intransigence. The Canadian response has been increasing resentment and anger. The U.S. has destroyed a lot of goodwill this side of the border.

At least half of the acid rain falling on Canada comes from the U.S. In some areas it runs as high as 70%. Wind currents carry some Canadian emissions to the U.S., but no more than 10% to 15% of acid rain falling in the U.S. can be blamed on Canada.

Most of the sulphur dioxide and nitrogen oxide emissions from the U.S. originate in the coal-burning electrical generating stations of the Ohio Valley. About two-thirds of the 30 million tonnes of sulphur dioxide spewing out of American smoke stacks comes from electrical utilities. Ironically, the oil crisis of the early 1970s caused the U.S. to convert many gas-fired generating stations to coal. Furthermore, much of the coal used in U.S. plants is high in sulphur content.

Some 1979 statistics listed the top 50 sulphur dioxide producing coal-fired power plants in eastern North America. Three belonged to Ontario Hydro; the other 47 were all American. Canadian plants produced 406,000 tonnes of sulphur dioxide that year, compared with 7,515,000 tonnes produced in the U.S. Some newer plants have had pollution control devices installed, but present U.S. legislation does not require the older facilities which are the main culprits to clean up their emissions.

Successive Canadian federal governments, and a couple of provincial governments, have tried to push the U.S. to tackle acid rain. Many of us think that Canada could have been much more aggressive over the past few years.

For a while, Canada tried to blackmail the U.S., by refusing to make reductions to our sources of sulphur dioxide and nitrogen oxide until they improved their record. Of course, that did not work. American political leaders were not particularly concerned about acid rain, to or from Canada. They were much more concerned about the cost, the economic dislocation that they thought would be caused by tackling acid rain.

Canada gave up that approach in 1984, and embarked on the plan to reduce our emissions by 50% by 1994. The hope was that unilateral action would shame the Americans into making a comparable commitment.

Susceptibility to shame is not a strong American characteristic. The Canadian program provided our allies in the States with extra ammunition. But others, from lobbyists for the coal industry and the electrical utilities to some politicians, poked holes in Canada's program. In 1986, Citizens for Sensible Control of Acid Rain, a lobby group financed largely by U.S. electricity and coal companies, spent $3 million U.S. fighting proposed acid rain controls in Congress. No other single lobby group has spent so much trying to influence U.S. legislators on any issue.

The official response continued to be avoidance. Until 1986, former President Reagan even refused to admit that acid rain was a serious environmental problem. Despite the monumental weight of scientific evidence about the damage caused by acid rain, the U.S. Government maintained that more study was needed before any action would be taken.

The Canadian churches have pushed their American counterparts to get involved, and to recognize acid rain as a major stewardship issue. In January 1984, the Canadian churches brought representatives of the major U.S. denominations to Toronto for a three-day intensive workshop on acid rain. It paid off—the Americans agreed to work with us to get U.S. action on acid rain.

Some of the American denominations have done education work with their congregations, and have encouraged their members to press politicians for action on acid rain. In June of 1986, I was asked to speak to an annual meeting of one of the synods of the Presbyterian Church in the U.S. I found them very receptive. I quite bluntly expressed Canadian frustration at the American inaction on acid rain. Responses to my speech indicated that we had some good allies in that room. People were embarrassed. Several speakers vowed to push their churches and their governments to take the problem much more seriously.

George Bush had always defended the Reagan administration's denial of scientific evidence linking acid rain to ecological damage. However, he discovered the environment during his 1988 election campaign. Suddenly, Bush was vowing that a Bush administration would take decisive action on acid rain. There are also some encouraging signs from Congress.

Whether real action happens will depend on how convinced Americans become that acid rain hurts them. In the meantime, American acid rain continues to fall on Canada unabated.

What we can do

Learn more about acid rain

There are some excellent sources of up-to-date information on the effects of acid rain, what is being done about it, and what needs to be done. The Canadian Coalition on Acid Rain brings together many different organizations, including environmental groups, labor unions, tourist associations, organizations of native peoples, and churches. It is the largest environmental coalition in Canada, a testimony to the seriousness with which people in many different parts of Canadian society view the acid rain problem. Joining the Coalition will give you access to reliable, detailed information, and will link you into a network that suggests specific actions for lobbying against acid rain.

Groups might show a very good film produced by the National Film Board of Canada, entitled *Acid Rain: Requiem or Recovery*. Several years ago, the American Administration banned distribution of this movie in the U.S., on the grounds that it was propaganda. The film takes about half an hour, and gives a concise overview of what causes acid rain and how it affects our ecosystem. It is available in all regional outlets of the National Film Board, and from some libraries.

Environment Canada has produced some helpful information, as have the provincial governments, particularly Ontario and Quebec. Writing to them directly or through your MP or MLA will get you a lot of literature.

Monitor Canadian governments and polluters

The federal government and governments in provinces that produce acid rain have all passed regulations to significantly reduce the emissions coming from polluting industries and utilities. But passing regulations and enforcing regulations are quite different matters. The Auditor-General in Ontario recently criticized the province's Ministry of the Environment for relying too greatly on data from the polluting industries themselves to monitor compliance with the regulations.

As the result of public pressure, politicians in Canada have taken some significant steps to address the acid rain problem. But that pressure has to be kept up. The federal government slipped in its commitment in early 1988 by taking a very weak position on nitrogen oxide emissions during a meeting of 30 countries in Europe. Like industries, governments need to be constantly monitored. Otherwise, they may assume that Canadians no longer care about acid rain. Writing to your MP and MLA keeps them aware of your concern.

The companies contributing to acid rain in Canada are mainly in Ontario, Quebec and the Maritime provinces. They too are sensitive to public opinion. Write and express your concern about acid rain and ask them for information on how they intend to comply with the regulations. They must be kept accountable.

Educate the United States

The federal government also has to be pressured about their action (or lack of it) in getting the United States to introduce legislation which will reduce acid rain-causing emissions. The Americans are our biggest problem. Prime Minister Mulroney liked to think that he could persuade President Reagan to take action because of the "special relationship" between the two leaders. In retrospect, it seems Reagan used that "special relationship" to delude Mulroney. Canadians have to communicate clearly and forcefully to our MPs, the Prime Minister, the Minister of the Environment, and the Minister of External Affairs that we consider acid rain serious enough to set aside the usual niceties of diplomatic relations with our big neighbor to the south, and to adopt a much tougher stand.

The federal government could more aggressively lobby the U.S. administration and Congress. They could initiate more public education in the U.S. to convince Americans that acid rain control is in their best interests too. There is also the possibility of legal action. Already, the Ontario Government has participated with several northeastern States to try and force the U.S. Environmental Protection Agency to act on acid rain. The federal government could attempt this route as well.

American politicians are not elected by Canadian voters, so they may pay little attention to us. Nevertheless, writing to them, and letting them know how angry Canadians are getting about U.S. inaction, cannot hurt. Many Americans have personal and business connections with Canada. Communication could increase the pressure to ensure that we remain good neighbors.

We could do some personal education and lobbying with American citizens. Many Canadians travel to the U.S. for business and vacations. Many Americans come to Canada for the same reasons. Such visits give us an opportunity to let Americans know personally how upset we are about *their* pollution killing *our* environment. Many Americans don't yet understand the seriousness of the problem. They might then be more prepared to pressure their politicians back home to take acid rain seriously.

One of my friends carries a sign in his car that says "STOP ACID RAIN." Whenever he passes a car with American licence plates, he flashes the sign at them. Their discomfort shows on their faces. That's a step in the right direction.

In some ways, acid rain tests our concern about the future of the earth. The issue has gotten lots of publicity.

Canadians can't claim that they don't know what it's about. The results are clearly documented in a great deal of scientific research.

If we are not concerned about acid rain, than we probably won't care about any of the other threats to creation. Acid rain is an issue that demands a response from us as Christians and as Canadians.

Resources for further information

The Canadian Coalition on Acid Rain, 112 St. Clair Ave. W., Suite 504, Toronto, ON, M4V 2Y3 (416) 968-2135

The Canadian Environmental Network, 1289 Station B, Ottawa, ON, K1P 5R3 (613) 563-2078

A Killing Rain—The Global Threat of Acid Precipitation, by T. Pawlick, Douglas & McIntyre Publ., 1984.

The Acid Rain Primer, 4th edition 1988, Pollution Probe, 12 Madison Ave., Toronto, ON, M5R 2S1 (416) 926-1907

We continue to produce toxic wastes that we don't know how to dispose of. In what condition are the many abandoned dump sites?

Toxic Wastes
Chemical killers

The term "toxic wastes" creates frightening images:
- boarded-up homes and abandoned playgrounds around Love Canal;
- trickling streams with who-knows-what poisons seeping out of the rock face above the Niagara River;
- barrels filled with unknown chemicals rusting behind deserted warehouses in countless communities across the country;
- wells, no longer safe to drink from, in rural settings far removed from urban industrial complexes.

Our modern consumer/industrial lifestyle poisons the water and earth that feed us. Toxic wastes are perhaps the most graphic illustration. Most of us seem to ignore the warning signals that we get. We shrug our shoulders, assuming that we can do nothing. Young people are not so complacent. Many of them are angry at the destruction they see. They are unconvinced that the benefits are worth the price. They know that they will inherit the mess, and have to pay for the clean-up.

The problem of toxic wastes is complex, but not unsolvable. Solving it will require a lot of ingenuity, persistence, energy and money.

The term toxic wastes has come to imply a wide variety of substances that are dangerous to humanity and the environment. Literally, toxic means poisonous. Most manufacturing processes produce wastes. Some are harmless, others are deadly. A broad estimate is that about 10% of all industrial wastes are hazardous.

To qualify as hazardous, the substance has to have one of the following characteristics:

- *ignitability* at a relatively low temperature
- *corrosiveness* (highly acidic or alkaline)
- *reactivity* (explodes or generates gases or fumes)
- *toxicity* (produces acute or chronic health effects)
- *radioactivity*
- *infectiousness*
- *carcinogenicity* (causes cancer)
- *mutagenicity* (damages the genes thus affecting future generations of humans, animals or plants)
- *teratogenicity* (causes birth defects)

These characteristics sound scary. The picture gets worse. Substances often have more than one of these attributes. In many waste disposals, substances may interact with each other, causing chemical reactions that produce new effects distinct from the initial wastes. To further complicate the situation, we simply do not know the long-term effects of many substances. We have been able to produce new chemicals

faster than we have developed means of testing them and
determining their impacts. Our society has tended to assume
that a substance is innocent until proven harmful. That principle may work in court rooms. But we are all paying a steep
price for that attitude in the environment.

A snapshot of some of the worst offenders

Dioxins pose a big problem in a small package

Though most of us have no idea what dioxins are chemi-
cally, we know that they are deadly. Their strength is awe-
some: 500 times as deadly as strychnine, 1000 times as
poisonous as cyanide. We also hear that they are showing up
all over the country—along hydro lines in New Brunswick
where they were used in herbicides, in herring gull eggs and
fish in Lake Ontario, and near an Alberta waste dump.

Dioxins are not produced intentionally. They have no
known beneficial use. They are an unintended by-product of
other substances, like some pesticides, herbicides and wood
preservatives. Dioxins are sometimes created accidentally
when some of these other products burn. The most lethal of
the 75 known types of dioxins is called TCDD. It has been
referred to by scientists as the most deadly chemical ever
produced.

The former Hooker Chemical Company, operating for
years on the U.S. side of the Niagara River, was a major
producer of a chemical of which TCDD is a by-product.
Tonnes of that chemical were buried in dump sites along the
Niagara River. One of the sites, called Hyde Park, apparently
holds about 3300 tonnes of the waste chemical containing
almost 2500 pounds of TCDD. Environment Canada scientists estimate that as little as 4 pounds of TCDD leaking into
the Niagara River would render Lake Ontario unfit as a
source for drinking water.

There is conflicting scientific evidence of how dioxins
affect humans. Dr. Douglas Hallett of the Canadian Wildlife

Service was the first to find TCDD traces in herring gull eggs: "We're not worried about people falling over dead at these levels, but about the long-term effects over a lifetime," he says.

Dioxins illustrate the difficult issues of toxic wastes. For instance, what would a "safe" dosage of TCDD be? At present, the testing equipment of the Ontario Ministry of the Environment can only detect TCDD at quantities larger than 0.2 parts per trillion. But the National Research Council of Canada considers a "virtually safe dose" of TCDD exposure much smaller than that. In other words, if we can detect dioxins at all, it's too much. According to the NRC's criteria, if we were to reach the point where Toronto's drinking water had 0.2 parts per trillion of TCDD, it would already be too late; the city would experience a cancer epidemic. Some people argue that with a chemical like TCDD, there is no such thing as a safe level—only varying risks.

Furthermore, who decides a "safe" level? Is this a job only for experts? Should the general public be involved? This points to some difficult and complex ethical issues. It shows how conflict can easily arise between industry, government, and environmental groups, and the general public.

Perhaps the churches have a role here. As Christians, we have no special expertise in the technical questions. But we can help to bring differing parties together, to discuss the issues. We can also raise long-term ethical perspectives. Through public dialogue, we may all become better informed and gradually move toward more of a consensus about how to handle toxic substances.

Abandoned waste dumps must be found and cleaned up

Dioxins grab the headlines. But thousands of other chemicals, less deadly but in much greater quantities, sit around in long-forgotten dump sites or behind abandoned factories. In 1979, an Ontario Government survey found 800 previously unknown dump sites. Researchers estimated that there were still another 2000 to 3000 unrecorded sites in southern Ontario alone. We don't even know where they are, let alone how much of a health and environmental threat they pose.

The small town of Mercier, southwest of Montreal, is in one of the prime vegetable and milk producing areas of Quebec. During a five year period ending in 1973, millions of gallons of liquid industrial wastes were dumped in an old gravel pit just outside of town. It gradually seeped into underground streams. By 1982, groundwater below 12 square miles of farmland in this area was considered permanently contaminated. The chemical concentrations in the water were 1000 times higher than allowed by federal drinking water standards. Over 8000 people were told by the provincial government not to drink the water from their wells.

If we have problems here in Canada, the situation in the U.S. is close to a disaster. Or perhaps they are just more aware of the problems because they have done the surveys to find out where the dump sites are. In Canada, we haven't done that kind of research. We seem to think that what we don't know can't hurt us.

In the U.S., an estimated 378,000 waste sites require corrective action. Of these, 10,000 presently pose a serious threat to people's health. At the moment, the U.S. Environmental Protection Agency has fewer than 1000 on its priority list for clean-up. During the first five years of its major campaign on toxic wastes (1980-85), the EPA only cleaned up six sites—and not very well, according to critics.

As I write this, the morning paper has a front page article about one of the largest hazardous waste dump sites in the eastern U.S. located in Niagara Falls, N.Y. It apparently contains 70 times as much toxic wastes as the infamous Love Canal dump. The frightening part of the story is that a whole maze of storm sewers run within a few hundred yards of the dump. The potential for leakage into the Niagara River grows daily. Even more frightening, the operator of the dump wants to double the size of the dump and take in more wastes!

In Saskatoon, some deep wells were used from 1963 to 1977 to dispose of hazardous chemical wastes. There is concern now that chemicals leaching from these wells may contaminate the ground water under the city.

Every province has its share of horror stories. A report in British Columbia stated that the lower Fraser River is "a filthy mess of illegal dumping and toxic wastes piling up for 25 years." When a recycling company in the province went bankrupt in 1978, it left an estimated 100,000 to 150,000 gallons of hazardous wastes in leaking barrels sitting in a couple of fields in a Vancouver suburb.

We keep producing toxic wastes

The problem of toxic wastes is not limited to chemicals created in the past and stored in now-forgotten sites. Each year we produce more. The federal government estimates that between 3 and 4 million tonnes are generated each year in this country. That's a lot of new dangerous garbage added to what we already have.

Almost every type of industry produces hazardous wastes. Lethal wastes come from pesticide manufacturers, forestry and agriculture. Toxic metal wastes are produced by smelting companies, petroleum refining, printing ink production, electrical appliance manufacturers, paint production and the pharmaceutical industry. A variety of organic chemical wastes that pose particularly difficult disposal problems are created by the plastics, electronics, aerospace and chemical industries.

Nobody knows just how much hazardous waste is created in Canada each year. Or where it is being produced. Or what is happening to it. Getting some answers to these questions is at least a starting point in designing strategies for cleaning up. Governments and industry have been slow to search for such answers. They know that not only is the search costly, but dealing with the products of the search will be even more expensive.

It appears that liquid and solid hazardous wastes are being disposed of in a variety of ways.

Some are burned or buried by companies on their own property. Questions arise—how safe are the emissions from their incinerators? How impermeable are their dump sites?

Other wastes are taken to private incinerators or municipally-owned landfills. These are, at least, the legal disposal means. The nightmare of the hazardous waste is the unknown quantity that is disposed of clandestinely in unapproved locations, poured into streams or sewers, or trucked to municipal dumps with no warning that they are hazardous.

A 1980 study in the Maritimes estimated that 65% of hazardous wastes in Prince Edward Island, Nova Scotia and New Brunswick were disposed of in unacceptable ways. Much of it was dumped completely untreated into municipal landfills and dumps. Many companies put hazardous wastes directly into sewers.

Toxic rain adds a new horror

You've heard of acid rain. In the future, you will be hearing even scarier stories about something called "toxic rain."

Researchers are just starting to realize that a great deal of our exposure to toxic chemicals comes not through water but through the air. Industrial smokestacks and the incineration of garbage send toxic chemicals high into the atmosphere. Like acid rain, they can travel for hundreds of miles before falling to the earth. When they fall in agricultural areas, they contaminate the soil and are absorbed into the fruit and vegetables that we eat.

What toxic wastes do to our health

I suspect that there would be a deafening outcry over toxic wastes, if it weren't for one of their basic characteristics: their effects rarely show up immediately. Cancers usually do not appear until at least 20 years after contact with the cancer-causing agent. Some effects may even jump a generation. They damage the parents' genes, and surface only in birth defects or other problems for the children or grandchildren.

The study of the effects of chemical wastes on human health is a relatively new field. Unfortunately, the laboratory where we learn most is human life.

A researcher studying the health of people living around Love Canal came up with some frightening statistics. She found that miscarriages and birth defects were three times as frequent as the rate for other parts of the Niagara Falls community. Convulsions, cancer, heart disease, respiratory diseases, skin disorders, bone problems—all occurred with greater frequency around the Love Canal than in neighboring areas.

We have similar problems on this side of the border. Residents living near the Upper Ottawa Street landfill in Hamilton, Ontario, became concerned about health effects resulting from burning wastes. They conducted their own research. Comparing the health of residents near the site with others living a few miles away, they found that sore throats occurred almost 14 times as often, colds 9 times as often, earaches 15 times, abnormal bleeding 5 times, and skin rashes over twice as frequently.

What is being done

In Canada, we need to do a great deal to clean up our toxic waste problems. But some things have started.

Alberta built the first facility in the country to destroy and dispose of toxic wastes. The Alberta Special Waste Treatment Centre is located near Swan Hills, about 250 kilometres northwest of Edmonton. It cost $50 million to build, and was a joint government/private venture.

The centre does a number of things with the wastes that it receives. These include physical/chemical treatment, stabilization, and incineration. Neutralized solid wastes are put in a covered landfill cell. Treated waste water is put in deep wells.

Ontario probably has the most acute problem with toxic wastes. The industrial heartland in the southern part of the province has hundreds of long-forgotten dumps. At the same time, industry continues to produce major quantities of hazardous wastes.

The Ontario Ministry of the Environment has developed an inventory system that should help us learn where the wastes are, who is producing them, and where they are going.

A provincial crown corporation is also developing strategies to handle toxic wastes. The Ontario Waste Management Corporation (OWMC) was formed in 1981 to construct a large waste disposal facility on the banks of the Grand River. But the site was chosen, not because it was the most appropriate, but because the government already owned the land. Local residents and farmers around South Cayuga knew that old gas wells on the site would allow buried wastes to seep into the river. The land also flooded every spring. It undermined confidence in government to learn that even with all their experts, they apparently didn't know basic information about the land which any local resident could have told them.

The OWMC backed down and returned to square one. They decided to research the most up-to-date technological solutions to toxic waste disposal, and come up with a plan for Ontario.

The OWMC's major effort has run into problems. OWMC proposed a large toxic waste facility to destroy some wastes, bury others, and store the rest above ground. They researched a variety of possible locations.

On the surface, their proposal sounded good. OWMC's glossy literature described the state-of-the-art technology. It looked impressive. But a small coalition of local citizens and groups, including members of some of the area churches, raised some fundamental and not easily dismissed questions. They see problems with the OWMC proposal, with its size and its disposal methods. The citizens' Toxic Waste Research

Coalition (TWRC) objected to having one large disposal facility in the province rather than several smaller ones. Having regional facilities would dramatically reduce the risks of transporting of toxic wastes across the province. Accidents on the highways are a major potential hazard, and are almost impossible to prevent.

The Coalition also raised questions about the wisdom of burying any toxic wastes. No one can guarantee that buried wastes will never leak. Furthermore, new technologies are being developed all the time. Some of the wastes being buried, because they cannot be destroyed with today's technology, might be with tomorrow's technologies.

A fundamental argument of this citizens' group is that whatever model we adopt, it must push industry to reduce the creation of wastes at the source. That is the only realistic long-term solution. We can't eliminate the creation of toxic wastes in the foreseeable future. But we can encourage industry to produce fewer hazardous wastes, to make more use of recycling technologies, and to take greater responsibility for the safe destruction and disposal of the remainder.

For me, one of the encouraging and hopeful aspects of the toxic waste situation in Canada is that public corporations have been mandated to find answers, while citizens actively challenge those corporations and come up with their own alternate proposals. Out of this ferment could eventually come the best possible solution. But pressure needs to be applied on the provincial governments. We will accept nothing less than the best and safest solution. The South Cayuga fiasco illustrates how readily governments will compromise principles to save money. That kind of attitude is both shortsighted and poor economics. The eventual costs of failing to deal adequately with toxic wastes today will be even heavier tomorrow.

Dealing with our own toxic wastes is only part of the problem. As with acid rain, we still have the Americans to contend with. Leaking U.S. dumps could affect millions of

Canadians who get their drinking water downstream from the Niagara River, where the heaviest concentration of dump sites exists.

Trying to get the U.S. to clean up their toxic waste dumps along the Niagara River has been an exercise in extreme frustration. Part of the problem relates to the U.S. approach to environmental issues. Everyone there seems so frightened by the economic costs of tackling these issues that they devote their time, energy and money to proving that *they* are not responsible. U.S. courts are filled with litigation cases, trying to establish whose responsibility a particular problem is. Confrontation seems to be the name of the game.

Granted, the costs of cleaning up toxic wastes in the U.S. will be horrendous. But their society has benefitted, over the years, from the substances of which these wastes are a by-product. Since the Americans have not paid adequately until now for proper handling of these by-products, they now have to pick up the tab.

Canada has pushed the U.S. to dig up the toxic wastes buried in dump sites near the Niagara River, truck the material farther inland so it cannot get into international waterways, and then dispose of it properly. So far, the U.S. Environmental Protection Agency has only suggested strategies like better containing the wastes in their present locations.

How do we adequately express our outrage to a neighboring country with whom we have historically had friendly relations? How do we force them to clean up, for their sake as well as ours? Our health and, the health of future generations, depends on finding effective answers to these questions.

What we can do

Learn more about toxic wastes
This is not always easy. Some good books describe the problems quite succinctly. One of the better ones, about the Ontario situation, is called *Chemical Nightmare: The Unnec-*

essary Legacy of Toxic Wastes, written by John Jackson and Phil Weller, two long-time environmentalists. Jackson is currently involved with the Toxic Waste Research Coalition raising questions about the disposal facility proposed by the Ontario Waste Management Corporation. The TWRC has produced a useful video on toxic wastes, entitled *The Turnaround Decade.*

Some environmental groups across Canada have researched and developed proposed solutions to the toxic waste problem. Pollution Probe has been active in the struggle to get the U.S. to clean up the dump sites leaking wastes into the Niagara River. They have good resources on the subject.

Environment Canada and some of the provincial governments also have produced material worth seeing. The problem with government publications, on an environmental time bomb like this, is that you have to read them with a rather critical eye. Governments are not much further ahead than the rest of us. But governments are naturally very nervous about the electorate. They realize what an explosive political issue drinking water contaminated with toxic wastes would be. So their publications are likely to downplay the issue, to try to reassure us that all that needs to be done is being done.

The same holds for industry. Some companies have taken commendable steps to reduce the amount of toxic wastes being produced by them, and to dispose responsibly of what does exist. But too often industry's primary principle has been to make a profit while avoiding public controversy. Concerns about the environment fall into the category of potential public relations nightmares. Therefore, any material you receive from industry may give you some helpful information, but try also to get perspectives from people in other areas. Environmental groups and universities are good sources of data about toxic wastes.

But the most important information on the subject is not written down anywhere. We know relatively little about the actual impact on the ecosystem and on human health of many toxic chemicals that exist in our environment. Many effects will take years to show up. It is hard to get research money for *suspected* problems.

A lot of information about potential problems within our own communities is lying around unrecognized because nobody has looked for it. Municipal councils are more concerned about visible potholes in the streets than about finding out what a now-abandoned fertilizer plant did with its wastes, or what the chemical plant on the edge of town is doing with present wastes. Many insidious and potentially lethal secrets have been buried around our communities, or dumped down our sewers.

Before we can seriously seek answers to the problem of toxic wastes, we need to know what kinds of questions to ask. It is difficult to approach such a problem alone. Organizing a small group of concerned citizens could be a first step.

Perhaps someone trained in chemistry, biology or environmental sciences would be interested, and could help. You do not have to have a university; a high school science teacher may be just the person you need. One of the local municipal councillors might have enough foresight to see this as an issue important to the community's long-term health. A public health nurse or a local doctor might provide medical awareness. And hopefully, members of local churches can be convinced that this is one way to demonstrate their concern about the future of God's creation.

Pressure for government and industry action

Governments and industry could be doing a great deal more than they are to study the threats posed by toxic wastes. They could mount aggressive programs to deal with wastes. But they have not—so far. Perhaps the slow effect of many of these chemicals leads them to think that their employees, or their voters, are not affected. The victims do not yet know that they are victims, and may be nowhere near the source of the problem when they finally do realize it. They are in no position to place much pressure on government or industry.

The pressure—if there is to be any—must therefore come from us. Raising the problem of toxic wastes to a higher priority on the political agendas of our governments is in all our best interests. This means learning as much as we can, to be in a position to ask for specific action, and not to be intimidated by the facile answers. It also means providing public education to generate more public interest.

Industry has a long history of resistance to government regulation on the environment. It seems that governments must take a much more aggressive role. The voluntary action by industry has been too little, too late.

Industry was ingenious enough to develop countless new chemicals for manufacturing purposes. It should be equally capable of figuring out ways to dispose of them safely. It should also be able to develop production processes that do not require as many deadly chemicals. Reducing the toxic wastes at their source is the most promising long-term solution to this problem.

There is also a vast potential for reuse and recycling of many chemicals, to keep them from entering the environment as wastes.

Some companies are developing new approaches to reducing their wastes. Not only is it good for the environment, but it also saves them money. However, in relation to the magnitude of the problem, these efforts are merely scraping the surface.

What will propel industry to assume this responsibility and to take some visionary leadership? Most horror stories in the media depict industry as doing all it can to disclaim any responsibility for environmental problems. The threat of closing plants and throwing people out of jobs is also a common response to the threat of environmental regulations. Yet there have been many situations where companies acted responsibly to deal with a problem of toxic wastes; the story never made the papers. So we need to commend publicly those industries that do make an effort to reduce toxic wastes.

But are those few efforts by a few companies enough to avoid disasters down the road?

We might start by pressing companies in our own communities to do more to reduce wastes. Managers and workers from those companies are active members of many churches. Sponsoring some dialogues within the congregation, between people concerned about the problem of toxic wastes and representatives of these companies, could lead to some lively exchanges. It could express a clear signal by the community of real concern about the future. Companies like to see themselves as responsible community citizens. Local pressure could have an effect.

Change our own lifestyles

Companies often defend their own actions by arguing that toxic chemicals are necessary if our society wants to continue its present standard of living. There is some truth to that defense. In many ways, the demands that we make for a material, effortless lifestyle are linked to products whose manufacture involves toxic chemicals. How do we sort out what we should use and not use, which are good products and which are environmentally harmful? And is that even a worthwhile exercise? After all, the toxic waste problem will not go away because a few individuals stop using certain types of paints or cut down on dry-cleaning.

This is not an either/or situation, *either* systemic change *or* personal lifestyle change. *Both* have to change. There is an intricate link between industrial practices and the social demands that feed those industries. We can make lifestyle changes that will help. But, since the vast majority of toxic wastes in our environment come from manufacturing processes, not from individual activity, we can have much more of an impact at that systemic level than we can by depending on individual lifestyle changes.

Yet in at least one area, individual activity can have a more significant effect. Toxic wastes are part of a larger problem facing our society—the growing garbage crisis. We are producing too many wastes, of too many different kinds. Toxic is just one variety of those wastes, albeit one of the most dangerous. As individuals and communities, we can make a significant difference by reusing and recycling more of our own wastes. But that topic deserves a chapter of its own.

Resources for further information

Chemical Nightmare—The Unnecessary Legacy of Toxic Wastes, by John Jackson and Phil Weller, Between the Lines Publishers, 229 College St., Toronto, 1982

Silent Spring, by Rachel Carson, Houghton Mifflin Publ., NY, 1962

Ontario Toxic Waste Research Coalition, Box 35, Vineland Station, Ontario, L0R 2E0

Pollution Probe, 12 Madison Ave., Toronto, ON, M5R 2S1 (416)926-1907

Where will we put the garbage when present dump sites are full?
Will the garbage pile up in our own back yards?

Garbage
Problems piling up on us

Garbage is what we put out by the curb on "garbage day." It
magically disappears. Free. No matter how much there is or
what it is, we "put it in the garbage" and it is gone.

Such, at least, is the experience of the vast majority of us
living in cities and towns across this country. Anything that
we no longer need—the excess packaging from our shopping,
the leftovers from our meals—all goes in the garbage pail.
Once or twice a week, we put that pail or pails by the road
and people driving trucks take it all away. We don't think
twice about it. We are only bothered about the operation

when our garbage pail lid lands in a neighbor's shrub, and we have to spend five minutes looking for it!

Disposing of our garbage this way has become part of our modern way of life. Each adult Canadian produces an average of 1 kg of garbage a day. That makes for a total annual output of more than nine million tonnes! And that is just from our homes. Commercial and industrial sources create millions of tonnes more. Most of this is shipped off by our municipal garbage services. No fuss, no mess.

Until now.

An expression says, "The unexamined life is not worth living." A relevant paraphrase for us today might be that the unexamined lifestyle may no longer be possible to live. With our garbage, things are not what they seem. We are going to have to examine that simple activity of getting rid of the garbage, which we have taken so much for granted.

Because disappearing garbage does not just disappear. Some larger urban centres are already running out of places to dispose of their garbage. Other communities in the country will face the same problem before long. The costs of finding better solutions will destroy any illusions that getting rid of our garbage does not cost us anything.

The landfills that we have traditionally used are getting full. There is a shortage of new available sites; we are running out of places to put garbage.

In the past, we just dumped everything, all mixed up, into a landfill. Thus we have many forms of hazardous wastes buried among the regular garbage. Over the years we will find increasing contamination of streams and groundwater around these landfills. Rain seeping down through the garbage could carry persistent and dangerous chemicals into surrounding water systems.

Burning garbage used to be seen as a miracle cure for the problem. We now know of the toxic chemicals that go up in the smoke from big garbage incinerators, and that are left in the ash.

Getting rid of our garbage in the future will become not only much more of a nuisance than in the past, but a potentially dangerous nuisance.

The garbage crisis is mainly an urban problem at the moment. Farmers and other rural dwellers have traditionally disposed of their garbage on their own. They burn some of it, put the organic material into compost piles to use as natural fertilizer, and truck the rest off to county dumps. Because they have been more conscious than city folk that garbage doesn't magically disappear, they have developed systems to deal with most of it in ecologically sound ways. We can learn a few lessons from them. But they too could be doing more.

Toronto's dilemma—a case study

Toronto is Canada's largest municipality. It is also one of the first to face a garbage crisis. Toronto's experience may well be a sign of the future for other communities.

Toronto's problem comes from a combination of poor planning and a dramatic increase in the amount of waste. Complacency has been the historic attitude of the general public and municipal officials. Torontonians, like Canadians in general, believed in the disappearing garbage myth.

Metro Toronto residents have had good garbage disposal services. In my area of the city, we get a collection every Monday and Thursday with a special collection on Wednesday for large objects, construction materials and recyclable products. Many home renovations are going on in my area. I commonly see piles of old drywall or wood strapping waiting to get picked up on a Wednesday morning. It all goes, at no additional cost to the residents. The expense is hidden in our municipal tax bill, so people have no real sense of garbage pick-up costing anything.

Of course, households are not the only source of solid wastes. Industry, construction and commercial operations create a great quantity. In fact, the largest increase in the amount of solid waste sent to municipal landfills over the past few years appears to be coming from the private sector.

About 4.8 million tonnes of solid waste were collected in 1987 from Metro Toronto and the two smaller nearby regional municipalities of Durham and York. Industry recycled about 1.5 million tonnes (32%)—mainly metal from old cars and appliances. The remaining 3.3 million tonnes was disposed of in two landfill sites operated by Metro Toronto. A small amount was burned in an old, polluting incinerator.

In 1983, Metro Toronto had to dispose of only 1.8 million tonnes. That is an increase of 77% from 1983 to 1987—just four years. For the six years previous to 1983, the amount of garbage had remained fairly constant at around 1.8 million tonnes. Toronto has been so complacent about its waste disposal that officials can neither explain nor account for the dramatic increase.

Both present landfill sites are filling up. One, the Brock West landfill, will have to close by early 1991. It presently takes a little under half of Metro Toronto's solid wastes. The Keele Valley site takes over half of Metro Toronto's garbage. A variety of factors could either extend or shorten its lifespan. It may no longer be available as early as 1992.

Only the threat of having nowhere to put our garbage is getting attention, at last, from politicians. Programs for reduction, reuse, recycling and recovery of wastes, have been slow in getting off the ground. When curbside recycling programs are available, residents respond enthusiastically. But municipalities have lagged on such programs; even the programs planned are not very ambitious. At the present rate, any serious commitment to public education about the potential and means of waste reduction, reuse, recycling and recovery, is still a long way off.

What would happen if both Toronto's landfill sites closed, with no alternatives developed, and Toronto was still producing as much garbage? The municipality would be faced with a health, environmental and economic disaster.

Garbage collection would obviously not occur regularly because trucks would have no place to dump what they had collected. Garbage could pile up on curbsides. People would probably start disposing of their trash illegally in parks, ravines, parking lots, wherever. After all, garbage is not something that you want sitting around. Before long, it starts decomposing, harboring disease-carrying insects, and attracting animals. The potential health effects of a prolonged garbage crisis could be very serious.

Indiscriminate disposal of garbage could result in waterways getting contaminated. Rain seeping through the refuse would spread bacteria and hazardous chemicals. Air quality would deteriorate if people started burning their garbage illegally.

A garbage crisis would also have a major impact on the economy of the region. Companies would either have to pay exorbitant costs to ship their wastes great distances for disposal, or close. Much of the construction industry might have to suspend operations. Any eventual solutions would be exceptionally expensive, resulting in dramatic tax increases. That in turn would pose hardships for many people, whether they own a home or have their rent jacked up by the landlord to cover increased costs.

Most of the factors underlying Toronto's dilemma are present in other communities across Canada. If residents of those towns and cities do not wake up to the garbage crisis faster than Torontonians, they too will face similar problems before long.

Potential solutions and their limitations

Find more landfill sites

One option would be for us to do what we have been doing for years. We could continue burying our garbage in massive holes in the ground, or building mountains of garbage and covering them with earth.

But the Toronto situation illustrates that it will be increasingly difficult to find new locations for dumps. Our urban areas eat into prime agricultural land. There is enough public anxiety already about losing farm land to housing developments. People will not want to bury even larger tracts of it under garbage. There are a few pieces of land unsuitable for housing, agriculture, or commercial development—usually ravines, marshes or wildlife areas. But we are all becoming more protective of these few sections of undisturbed nature around our cities.

Citizens living near possible dump sites get understandably upset at suggestions that they might end up living beside a massive garbage pile. They don't just object to the smell, or the rising pile, but there would be all those huge dump trucks coming and going, creating new problems of heavy traffic. Add to this a growing awareness of environmental and potential health problems associated with dumps, and it's clear why few people would willingly accept a new landfill site next door. Politicians and municipal officials find it hard to convince anyone otherwise.

Some suggest that cities will just have to go farther afield to find new sites. This suggestion creates a number of economic and ethical problems. Transportation is a major cost in disposing of waste. If trucks have to go a long distance, then the costs to the municipality will skyrocket. Also, the farther you truck garbage, the greater the chances of accidents occurring.

But even beyond economics, we have to raise a serious ethical question. Is it fair to ask people outside the city to put up with the problems and risks of a dump handling garbage created by city dwellers? City people often have an illusion of vast tracts of land beyond the city border that are sparsely populated and, therefore, unused. Rural and northern people quickly respond that the land serves many purposes, for both human and non-human members of creation. It is not available for anything the cities might desire. Especially garbage dumps. The city created the garbage; the city should handle the garbage.

Finding new landfill sites to take our garbage is obviously not as easy as it once was. There are now good reasons to question whether landfill is a good option even if we could find sites. The waste of valuable resources that could be recycled represents an economic loss both from not recovering them, and from having to use more non-renewable resource to produce new products. Also, environmental problems could result from hazardous wastes being mixed into the regular garbage and dumped into massive sites.

All in all, garbage dumps ain't what they used to be. Nor should they be.

To burn or not to burn?

There is a hot (pardon the pun) debate going on about the merits and hazards of building incinerators to burn garbage. Both sides present convincing arguments with statistics to back up their positions.

I must say that my reaction at this point is to recommend supreme caution. Our past is littered with examples of jumping into new ventures precipitously before we had sufficient information on long-term environmental impacts. The size of the incinerators presently being built or proposed creates a political and economic momentum, causing projects to continue, even if serious problems surface. I believe it would be better to take enough time to research and consider the advantages and disadvantages *before* building incinerators.

Burning garbage is not a new idea. Humanity has done it from our earliest origins. The process got a big boost, however, in the 1970s. At that time, two different phenomena began emerging simultaneously. Forward thinkers started to realize that our growing cities would sooner or later encounter problems disposing of the increasing amounts of garbage. Burning seemed a great way to dispose of the massive volume of garbage that would be produced.

The other major development was the energy crisis. Suddenly, energy was no longer the cheap, constantly available commodity that we had taken for granted for so long. Interest grew in searching for new sources.

One possible source was to burn garbage to generate energy. This seemed an ideal solution for urban centres or large facilities. Their garbage could be burned to heat water or produce steam. The hot water or steam could then heat large buildings at much lower cost than by burning fossil fuels like oil, gas or coal. The application particularly appealed to big companies, hospitals, and shopping malls. They could get rid of their garbage and save on their energy bills at the same time.

Alternately, the burning of garbage could create steam to generate electricity. Electricity had even greater flexibility than hot water or steam. It could be sent greater distances and have wider uses. Municipalities started considering this idea.

A reorganization of responsibilities in the provincial bureaucracy in Ontario shows how attractive this form of waste disposal became. Responsibility for "energy from waste" programs was transferred from the Ministry of the Environment to the Ministry of Energy. The change demonstrates again the subtle ways in which economics often wins out over the environment. The focus became the energy-creation potential of incinerating wastes. Environmental considerations were the add-on, rather than the focus.

The concept of building big incinerators got a substantial push from the energy crisis. Some communities already had incinerators, but few had energy-producing components attached. Incineration seemed to be the ideal way to dispense with our garbage.

In the late 1980s, as the garbage problem has grown, the idea of building incinerators seems to be gaining an almost unstoppable momentum. A report on Toronto's garbage crisis by Metro Councillor Richard Gilbert recommends incinerators as being friendly to the environment.

State-of-the-art incinerators can control the vast majority
of hazardous emissions, Gilbert argues. Now Toronto is
contemplating building two large incinerators, to be located
on the waterfront near my neighborhood. These, apparently,
will emit 8.6 micrograms (a microgram is a billionth of a
kilogram) of dioxins for each tonne of garbage that they burn.
That certainly compares favorably with the 13,867 micrograms of dioxins per tonne of garbage burned that spewed
from Toronto's old incinerator, until it closed in 1988.

Gilbert also addresses the hazards of the ash left over after
the garbage is burned. He quotes the Swedish Environmental
Protection Board, that putting incinerator ash in landfills
poses fewer environmental hazards than landfilling regular
garbage. He argues, therefore, that ash is not a big worry.

Gilbert's report notes that incineration is much more
expensive than landfill. Construction and operation of a good
incinerator in Toronto would cost about $100 for each tonne
of waste it burns during its lifetime. This compares with about
$40 per tonne for present landfill dumps. However, if an
incinerator also produces energy to heat buildings or as
electricity, the costs become quite comparable. Gilbert therefore sees incineration as an attractive option for the garbage
crisis.

But not everyone is convinced.

Pollution Probe, for one, has some serious reservations
about incineration. They also provide scientific data to back
up their argument.

Pollution Probe published a report in May 1986 (and
updated it in March 1988) called *Up The Stack (and Into the
Foodbasket): Dioxins and Incineration*. According to the
report, we may be seriously at risk from dioxins (and the
closely related chemical furans) which are transported
through the air, and fall on our orchards, pastures and food
crops.

A couple of years ago, newspapers reported disturbing
results of a study on samples of food grown in Ontario. The

food had unexpectedly high concentrations of dioxins and furans, surpassing Ontario's Acceptable Annual Intake standard.

As reported by Pollution Probe, the fruit analyzed had dioxin and furan concentrations 37.8 times higher than Ontario's Acceptable Annual Intake. Milk samples were 19.3 times higher; meat and egg samples 9 times higher. For the total dietary intake, this amounts to exposures to dioxins and furans at many times the level recommended by Ontario's Acceptable Annual Intake standards.

How does our food get contaminated with poisons like dioxin? The poisons travel through the air and fall on our foodlands. According to the Federal Expert Advisory Committee on Dioxins, the largest source of dioxins poisoning the Canadian environment is incineration. Most dioxins come from the burning of municipal garbage, but industrial waste incineration is also a major source. So maybe there are significant environmental reasons to question the wisdom of building incinerators as a principal means of solving our garbage crisis.

But incinerator proponents maintain that the newest technology will allow a dramatic reduction in dioxin emissions.

The Pollution Probe report throws cold water on overly enthusiastic expectations. Pollution Probe researchers indicate that the majority of claims about improved emission controls refer to systems called precipitators or baghouses. These remove *particles* of pollution in the smokestack. However, about three-quarters of the dioxins and furans going up the stack are not attached to particles at all but are in gaseous or vapor form.

We could control dioxins better by designing incinerators to do a more complete job of combustion. But ultimately, it is impossible to burn garbage without creating dioxins and furans. If we already have too many poisons in the environment, building garbage incinerators across the country will only compound the problem.

Hazardous emissions coming out the stack are not the only reason for Pollution Probe's caution. New questions are being raised about the toxicity of the ash left over after the burning process. Another Pollution Probe publication, *Garbage Incineration: Lessons from Europe and the United States*, indicates that there may be more problems with the ash than we thought.

Incineration sounded good, as an answer to our developing garbage crisis. But the more we learn about incineration, the more reasons emerge for sober second thoughts. Now is the time for such caution, before we spend hundreds of millions of dollars building potential environmental nightmares. If we jump too quickly, we may find ourselves burdened with extremely expensive mistakes. Faced with a choice between mothballing huge white elephants, or using them and putting up with the environmental damage, I fear which our society would probably choose—if past performance is any guide.

A huge economic and political investment in building incinerators may also undercut a commitment to what I believe is a more effective long-term solution to our garbage crisis—the four Rs: reduction, reuse, recovery and recycling.

Putting the four Rs to work

Ecological systems have a basic property that we seem to have forgotten. They do not produce unusable garbage. The fallen tree, animal droppings, a dead fish, all decompose. Their elements become a source of growth for some other life. The entire system is interconnected. All parts are involved in an elaborate process of continuous recycling. Such systems are sustainable. They can continue to function and thrive indefinitely.

Our garbage crisis is a visible sign that humanity's way of operating is no longer sustainable or ecologically sound. We create vast quantities of wastes which we do not reuse. Our ways of disposing of these wastes have become a serious threat to our health and to the environment as a whole.

Another approach to dealing with our waste problem has a lot to commend itself. The four Rs are reduction, reuse, recycling and recovery. This approach minimizes the amount of garbage that is produced. It then reintegrates the majority of waste that is created back into our ecosystem as useful elements. This approach would be much more sustainable than our present practices. It is also likely to be more economically viable over the long term

Reduction is the starting point. Let us stop creating so much waste in the first place.

To make a really significant shift in how our society deals with its waste problem, we are going to have to start with changes at the front end. As consumers, we are part of the problem, and part of the solution.

As one example, think of how packaging affects our purchasing decisions. We tend to buy whatever looks most attractive on the store shelf. Manufacturers, catering to this impulse, put a lot of money into fancy packaging.

When we have the option of choosing between goods of equal quality, we should make a habit of selecting the one with the least packaging. In the grocery market, we could take the loose produce, rather than those that were already packaged on foam or wrapped in plastic. A really radical step would be to take our own bags, rather than use new ones each time at the store!

But people often complain that they have no choice. They have to buy heavily packaged products, because that is all that's available. Manufacturers also have to change, to produce less packaging. The companies will protest that the consumer demands fancy packages. It becomes a chicken-and-egg debate.

It obviously is not a matter of either/or. We must change our buying habits as consumers; we must *also* demand that companies change their approaches to packaging. In our economic system, companies are influenced primarily by what sells. If we stop buying heavily packaged goods, companies will change. We have to ensure that change is in their economic self-interest. In the meantime, it certainly would not hurt to let manufacturers know our opinions. Write to the company, or tell the manager of the store where you are shopping. Initially, they may disregard your comments, or claim that changes are beyond their control. But if your message is reinforced over and over, by word, and by unspent dollar, they will listen.

Industrial processes offer many opportunities for reducing the amount of waste that is created. Companies seem to have an endless capacity to create new products for us to spend money on; they should apply as much ingenuity to developing improved manufacturing processes. One reason that research dollars have not gone into waste reduction, is that so far we have made it too easy for these companies to dispose of their garbage cheaply. As waste disposal becomes more expensive, it will be in their interests to have less waste to get rid of.

Unfortunately, higher waste disposal costs would also have to be accompanied by increased surveillance, to guard against illegal and clandestine dumping. Some people, and some companies, have so little respect for the environment that they would prefer to pollute it than to pay more, either for responsible disposal or for reducing waste production. I dream of the day when people would become as outraged about that immorality as they do now about issues of sexual morality.

Reuse refers to the using again, in its original form, something which we might have thrown out. Refillable bottles, plastic bags, jars, many kinds of containers could all be employed again. We would save in two ways. We—or society generally—would not have to pay for the disposal of that container. Secondly, we would not have to pay for a new one!

On another level, we can encourage reuse of many products by sharing them with others. In my neighborhood, Saturday morning yard sales are fun and profitable entertainment. They also decrease the amount of waste we generate. Rather than throw things in the garbage, we put them into a yard sale. Invariably, someone will buy the item, and use it again. It is a great way to have products reused, make a little money, meet your neighbors and help preserve the environment, all at the same time. If you are not into yard sales, take the goods to a second-hand store, to Goodwill Industries, or to a Salvation Army depot. In virtually every community, some facility would gratefully receive your leftovers.

Industries could also reuse much of their waste. In some cases, it might involve a bit of redesigning. For instance, some wooden pallets, on which merchandise is stacked, are manufactured for use only once. That is a terrible waste. We not only cut more trees to produce new pallets, but we use more energy destroying the old ones when they are thrown in the garbage. Reusable pallets make much more sense. They might cost more initially, because they would have to be designed to stand up to the wear of repeated use. But when you add up all the costs of manufacturing and destroying the disposable variety, reuse starts making economic as well as environmental sense.

Recycling has a tremendous potential for reducing the volume of garbage. Many household products can already be recycled. Most people were first introduced to recycling

Response to Toronto's Blue Box recycling program has been overwhelming. We can all do our part to combat the garbage crisis.

through the disposal of old newspapers. In our area, the Scouts held a "paper drive" a couple of times a year. We would all dutifully put out the papers that we had remembered to save.

We have come a long way since then. An increasing number of communities have regular recycling programs where newspapers, tin cans, and glass are picked up each week. In the area where I live, the city wanted to see how people would respond to the opportunity to recycle. We were all given durable blue plastic boxes to put by the curb every Wednesday, filled with our week's supply of glass, tin and newspaper. The response has been overwhelming. When I walk down my street on a Wednesday morning, at least 85% of the homes have their filled blue boxes sitting out front. The program has now been expanded to include the whole city.

Some environmental groups, governments and industries are researching means of recycling more household materials, including corrugated cardboard, plastics, textiles, batteries, and some chemicals.

There are many commercial and industrial opportunities for recycling. This can become particularly critical when we have hazardous wastes to deal with. Companies that find ways to recycle wastes—especially hazardous wastes—not only avoid the environmental and economic costs of disposal, they also reduce their expenses by not having to buy fresh supplies of the product.

Recovery is a variation on recycling. Recycling depends on the original user to sort products, keeping cans and glass separate from the rest of the garbage for pick-up. Recovery involves trying to retrieve, from mixed garbage, materials for reuse. Steel cans, for example, can be pulled out of other garbage by magnets. Research continues on developing ways to recover other valuable material. Another form of recovery happens when energy is produced through processes of waste disposal. China now meets some of its energy needs by producing methane gas from human and animal wastes.

The four Rs will not solve all of our garbage problems overnight. But they have more advantages for our health, environment and economy than most of the other options. Of course, there will be difficulties along the way. But if we put as much money and time into this approach as we are considering for building massive incinerators and developing huge new landfill sites, we could go a long way towards reducing the amount of garbage that will finally have to be disposed of.

What we can do

Get information

The garbage problem is very much a local environmental issue. It starts in our own homes. We can do many things about it right where we live.

Our neighborhoods and communities also have to make some practical decisions. The Public Works department used to receive little interest from either citizens or municipal politicians. The garbage crisis may change that.

Information on what and how to recycle is available from some conservation and environmental groups across the country as well as some provincial governments. Learn how you can change practices in your own life and home. It takes some energy and reorganization, but the benefits for your own situation, as well as for the environment, are worth it.

Encourage healthy government programs

Provincial and municipal governments have been slow to realize the dimensions of the coming garbage crisis. When they do wake up, they frequently jump for high profile, high-tech solutions. Politicians like to show off these projects.

As citizens we need to learn the strengths and weaknesses of the various options, so that we can pressure our municipal governments to choose approaches that will protect the environment. Because many decisions about waste management rest with our municipal governments, we can more easily become personally involved than with some other environmental problems. We can attend and make submissions to municipal council hearings. This is more effective if organized through a local citizens' group. In most places, citizens' groups are the most effective voice in the community.

Municipal governments can also play a major role in pushing industry to develop more ecologically sensitive ways of handling their wastes. Some companies have been very responsible in dealing with their wastes and researching new technologies for reduction and recycling. Others are not so concerned. The threat of fines for "crimes against the environment," or of adverse publicity, might get environmental protection higher on their list of priorities.

Provincial governments can encourage municipalities to get involved in major recycling programs through incentive grants and providing technical consultation. Call your provincial member of parliament; find out how much or how little he or she knows about options for waste disposal. Indicate that you are concerned.

Garbage is a problem today. Let us take informed and assertive action now before it gets a lot worse.

Resources for further information

Contact the environmental groups in your area which have been involved in providing information on recycling and waste disposal.

Request information from your provincial Ministry of the Environment.

Garbage Incineration: Lessons from Europe and the United States, Pollution Probe, 12 Madison Ave., Toronto, ON, M5R 2S1, 1987

The Solid Waste Crisis and Some Solutions, Report by Metro Toronto Councillor Richard Gilbert, Toronto City Hall, 1988

Up the Stack (and Into the Foodbasket): Dioxins and Incineration, Pollution Probe, 12 Madison Ave., Toronto, ON, M5R 2S1, 1988

One worker takes radiation readings while two others work on a ruptured pressure tube in the nuclear power plant at Pickering.

Nuclear Power
Unforgiving technology

Public skepticism about the safety of nuclear power plants has increased considerably since the accidents at Three Mile Island and Chernobyl. We are told that such accidents could never happen in Canada. Officials from government, Atomic Energy of Canada Ltd. (the manufacturer of the CANDU reactor), and the provincial utilities generating nuclear power, Ontario Hydro in particular, all extol the safety of the CANDU reactor.

Yet the reactors themselves—even if they are as safe as their proponents claim—are only part of the total environmental concern. The nuclear fuel cycle, from uranium mining to the disposal of the spent reactor fuel, involves many environmental questions, both present and long-term.

The debate about nuclear power has been around in Canada and other countries for a long time. It will heat up again, because some see a great expansion of our nuclear power capability as the solution to the global "greenhouse effect," the warming of the earth's atmosphere. Fossil fuel burning power plants that release vast quantities of carbon dioxide are one of the major contributors to the production of greenhouse gases. Some people see nuclear energy as the answer.

It is not a good answer. In the chapter on the greenhouse effect, I describe why it won't be of much help at all in slowing the global warming. In addition, a vast expansion of nuclear energy programs would saddle us and many future generations with serious environmental problems.

There are some very dangerous types of garbage produced by different stages of the nuclear process.

The mining and milling of uranium produces vast quantities of radioactive tailings—discarded rock and ore. These tailings are just left sitting around in open reservoirs. Processing uranium to produce reactor fuel results in more low-level nuclear wastes, presently stored near Eldorado's plant in Port Hope, Ontario. Finally, after the fuel rods have completed their tasks in the reactors, they have to be stored, somehow. For a very long time. These high-level nuclear wastes remain radioactive for tens of thousands of years—longer than all recorded history! At the moment, they are stored in pools of water on the sites of nuclear reactors.

All of these wastes represent threats to human health and to the environment. It is perhaps the ultimate irresponsibility for us, in the interests of feeding our energy-greedy life style during these few decades in the latter part of the 20th century, to create radioactive wastes that will remain hazardous for up to a quarter of a million years.

The Costs of Nuclear Energy

Uranium mining and milling releases harmful substances

Years of research convincingly show that uranium miners suffer higher-than-normal levels of cancer from exposure to the low-level radiation in the mines. The Atomic Energy Control Board is charged with overseeing nuclear affairs in Canada. They published a report in 1982 showing that workers exposed to the present maximum permissible levels in Canadian mines for a 30-year period would experience about four times as much lung cancer as non-miners. A 1974 Ontario study indicated that uranium miners in Elliot Lake already had twice the normal cancer rate. The B.C. Medical Association, in a report published in 1980, entitled "The Health Dangers of Uranium Mining," predicted a steadily increasing number of radiation-induced cancers among Canadian uranium miners.

The culprit in all these studies is a colorless, odorless, tasteless gas called radon. While the uranium is undisturbed in the ground, relatively little of the cancer-causing radon gas escapes. But the mining process pulverizes the rock. The radioactive radon gas escapes into the mine atmosphere. The miners are exposed.

Saskatchewan mines have some of the richest concentrations of uranium in the world. At the Cigar Lake Mine, the average concentration of uranium in the ore is about 14%; it reaches 60% in some places. Most uranium mines around the world have concentrations of 0.5% to 2%. The high ore concentrations lead to high radiation levels. The Cigar Lake Mine has the highest radiation levels of any underground uranium mine in the world.

From the mine, the ore heads to the mill. Most of the rock that goes into a uranium mill comes out the other end as waste. Already, Northern Saskatchewan has over 24 million tonnes of solid waste. These wastes, or tailings, still contain about 85% of the total radioactivity in the original ore, as well as a number of heavy metals like arsenic, lead and copper that have their own poisoning effect on the environment.

Liquid wastes likely have an even greater impact on the environment, because they can so easily slip into water systems and be carried great distances. There are reports that contaminated water from the uranium mines in the Uranium City area of northern Saskatchewan has leached into Lake Athabasca.

Even the more modern containment reservoirs have a potential for spills. The Key Lake Mine has been touted as one of the most modern, safe and efficient uranium mines in the world. It was the site of a major spill in January 1984. Over 75 million gallons of radioactive water spilled out of a reservoir. Fortunately, the lake into which it flowed was not connected to any larger northern water system. Had the reservoir wall broken in another location, the radioactive spill could have drained into the Wheeler River, which is directly connected to the Churchill, one of Saskatchewan's most important river systems.

Environmental groups, native people, and churches in Saskatchewan have long raised concerns about the safety of uranium mining and the poor way in which radioactive wastes are handled. But the provincial and federal governments continue granting permits for the opening of still more mines. In 1987 and 1988, the Saskatchewan government gave approval for four new uranium mines, which will eventually more than double that province's uranium production.

Northern Ontario has its horror stories as well. Near Elliot Lake, over 80 million tonnes of radioactive wastes or mine tailings sit piled up on 1800 acres. Radioactive dust blowing off the piles washes into nearby streams. The Serpent River is so contaminated from these wastes that it can sustain no fish for over 80 kilometres downstream. Exposed mine tailings give off at least ten thousand times as much radon gas as the undisturbed ore.

Low-level wastes sit close to home

The substance that comes out of the mill is called "yellow-cake." This more concentrated product heads towards refineries like Eldorado Nuclear Ltd., in Port Hope on the shores of Lake Ontario. Here, yellowcake is turned into the fuel used in Canada's reactors. Yellowcake is a source of low-level radiation. So far there have been no major accidents in Canada during the shipping of yellowcake to Port Hope. There has been one yellowcake spill in North Dakota. The uranium came from Saskatchewan's Key Lake Mine. That one spill cost about $1 million to clean up.

Eldorado had been refining uranium for a long time before the hazards of the kinds of low-level wastes produced at the plant were recognized. Fill contaminated by Eldorado's wastes was used on many construction sites in Port Hope. A survey in 1976 found that one-third of the property in Port Hope had above-normal levels of radiation. Radioactive wastes had been used to fill in a ravine, on which a school was subsequently built. When it was discovered that students and teachers were exposed to levels of radon gas up to twenty times higher than those considered safe by the federal government, the school was closed.

For years, Port Hope has experienced an unhappy struggle between nuclear officials and citizens concerned about the effects of these wastes. The citizens have received endless run-arounds, trying to find out who is responsible for deciding on how Eldorado should dispose of its wastes. Sometimes the federal government, which has responsibility for most nuclear questions, seems to be supporting the citizens. But for the most part the government seems, to the people, to be protecting Eldorado.

The town itself is split three ways. Many people are concerned, and demand that a safe disposal facility be found away from populated areas and a long distance from the lake. Others maintain that Eldorado will do the right thing; these people are prepared to trust the experts from the company and the government who say that there is nothing to worry about. Many other citizens just don't want to talk about it. The problem is too close to home and too scary. On the one hand, Eldorado is a big employer in town. On the other hand, if the problem is real, it is going to affect their health, and their children's health.

Reactor safety draws doubt

This area of the nuclear debate is probably the most contentious. Officials in the Canadian nuclear industry defend the quality of the CANDU reactors that operate in Canada. They maintain that Canadian reactors are the best designed in the world and have the best operating record. People who raise concerns about reactor safety argue with conviction that no technology is infallible and that there are definite weaknesses about the CANDU reactor.

Nuclear technology is sometimes referred to as an "unforgiving" technology. It may be very sophisticated and very reliable and have very few accidents. But when it does have an accident, the consequences for humans and the natural environment can be catastrophic.

The worst nuclear accident so far (at least up to the time I write this!) was at Chernobyl. On April 25, 1986, a nuclear reactor exploded near that Soviet town. Radioactive debris covered the surrounding area. Clouds of radioactive particles spread across much of Eastern Europe and Scandinavia.

Within a few weeks, 31 people had died of the direct effects of the explosion. Scientists and medical experts predict that within a 315-mile radius, 10,000 people will die of lung cancer in the next decade. Over 135,000 people had to be evacuated from the Chernobyl region. About 66 square miles of some of the most productive farmland in the U.S.S.R. have been rendered unusable. In Scandinavia, hundreds of thousands of reindeer were declared unfit for consumption because their grazing areas were so contaminated. The herders of Lapland received more than $200 million in compensation from the Swedish government, but money will not pay for the loss of a traditional way of life hundreds of years old. After that accident, people around the world started looking more critically at their own country's nuclear programs.

Canadian officials cringe when they hear someone mention Chernobyl. They believe that there is no valid basis for comparing the Canadian situation with the Russian. Canadian nuclear officials have tried to reassure us that a Chernobyl disaster could not happen here. But are they right?

The Church and Society Committee of London Conference of the United Church of Canada decided to do some research. The Ontario Government had set up a Nuclear Safety Review after Chernobyl; the church committee got a bit of funding from the Review to hire a researcher. Their conclusion is summed up in the title of their article: *Chernobyl: It could happen in Canada.*

There are some major differences in design between Soviet and Canadian reactors, but there are also some important similarities. Both use pressure tubes made out of the same metal alloy to hold the uranium fuel in the reactors. The Chernobyl accident may have started with a break in one of the tubes. Such a pressure tube did split open in 1986 at the Bruce Nuclear Reactor near Douglas Point, Ontario. Ontario Hydro has found that the pressure tubes are wearing more quickly than engineers had anticipated, and the tubes are developing cracks. Several of Ontario reactors have been shut down recently, to replace cracked pressure tubes.

Ontario Hydro claims that because they use a different coolant, a CANDU reactor could not overheat like Chernobyl. Other nuclear experts are not so sure. Some U.S. scientists contend that a CANDU reactor might not melt down but it could burn up with equally devastating consequences.

Another difference from the Soviet reactors is that the CANDUs have large containment systems to catch any escaping radioactivity. They consist primarily of large concrete and steel bubbles constructed over the reactor. However, the Chernobyl blast was nearly 100 times greater than necessary to destroy the largest CANDU containment dome.

There will doubtless be ongoing debates about who is right. Are Canadian reactors safe or not? And what do we mean by safe? Even the nuclear industry admits that nothing is absolutely foolproof. So does safe mean that the risk of a major accident like Chernobyl is one in 100 years or 1,000 years or 10,000 years?

Are the benefits of nuclear power reactors worth the risks of possible accidents? That would be a more difficult question to answer if I thought that there were no alternatives. But we have learned a lot in recent years about how our society could live using energy in a much more efficient and less wasteful manner. With more attention paid to conservation, and to designing our buildings, cities and transportation systems to be more economical in the energy they use, we could live a very high quality of life without nuclear power. From a Christian ethical perspective, should we not be seeking to use energy more effectively rather than constantly producing more to meet our ever-expanding appetite?

Our civilization is getting to the point where we have to question whether we should follow a particular path just because it seems technically feasible. Nuclear power may be one of these areas. We know that we can generate electricity from nuclear reactors. But should we? Is it worth the risk?

High-level nuclear wastes last almost forever
Canada began developing nuclear reactors in the late 1940s. Now, over 40 years later, we still have no proven method of safely disposing of their highly radioactive wastes. How can we justify continuing to build and operate reactors when we have yet to find a way to handle their deadly wastes? Future generations who will have to look after these wastes for us will demand an answer to such a question. It should make us squirm.

California and the United Kingdom decided some time ago not to proceed with further expansion of nuclear power until a satisfactory disposal method is developed. We should consider similar action.

The spent fuel coming out of a nuclear reactor is referred to as "high-level" because of its extreme radioactivity. As I mentioned earlier in the chapter, the used fuel is suspended in large pools of water on the sites of Canada's reactors. That is only a temporary solution. The life-expectancy of most nuclear plants is about 30 years. Their wastes remain radioactive for many thousands of years. We need to find a long-term solution that will be safe, and leak-proof.

Atomic Energy of Canada Ltd. (AECL) has the responsibility for developing disposal technology. It has chosen to research only one option: drilling small cavities in granite formations deep under the earth's surface and burying the wastes there. AECL maintains that it has sufficient contact with research being conducted in other countries to avail itself of other disposal methods which might be developed there.

Residents in areas that have been suggested as possible disposal sites react angrily. One can understand their concern. Exposure to even a small amount of the waste could kill a person in seconds. There are already over 7000 tonnes of high-level wastes being stored by Ontario Hydro "temporarily." Each of the operating reactors at Ontario Hydro's Pickering plant produces another tonne *every five days*. Most of the places with the preferred type of rock formation are in northern Ontario. People living in the north are not crazy about the idea of having to live with radioactive wastes produced in the south to serve southern Ontario's energy needs.

What is being done

Research is going on regarding safe methods of disposing of both high-level and low-level nuclear wastes. The federal government and AECL have glossy brochures describing their efforts—particularly the Whiteshell research facility in Manitoba. There, AECL is digging experimental deep wells in bedrock to develop a process for storing the highly radioactive wastes from nuclear reactors. (The government has promised the people of Manitoba that even though the research is going on there, the ultimate dump site will not be in their province. That seems only fair since Manitoba does not produce any high-level nuclear wastes. They have no nuclear plants. The wastes that need permanent storing come mainly from Ontario Hydro, with its massive nuclear program. Smaller quantities of nuclear wastes come from a couple of other provinces.)

A government task force is looking into ways to store the vast quantities of low-level wastes generated by the Eldorado uranium refinery in Port Hope. Residents there have been pushing for years to have the wastes that have been dumped around the town properly disposed of. They are also concerned about where Eldorado will put their ever-increasing supply of wastes since the facility that they have been using is inadequate.

But at least these two kinds of wastes are getting some serious attention. Uranium mine tailings are not. Perhaps because most uranium mines are in remote northern areas of Saskatchewan and Ontario, there is less public concern. The problem is not on our doorstep.

The mining companies and the provincial government contend that their methods of storing the mine tailings are absolutely safe. They may be—for the next decade. But future generations will have to deal with the mess if these assurances turn out to be wrong.

Finally, the whole question of nuclear safety continues like a recurring nightmare. The government reviews have generally concluded that nuclear power in Canada is safe enough—whatever that means. Church bodies have pressed for years for a full-scale public inquiry into nuclear power. So far, no federal government has been prepared to convene such an inquiry. The fiscal and political commitment that governments have to nuclear power in this country is so massive that they probably cannot conceive of Canada phasing out its nuclear program. But Sweden is doing just that.

What we can do

Citizen groups have found it difficult to make much headway against the nuclear industry. The private companies involved, the crown corporations, the provincial governments and the federal government present a solid front of unwavering belief in and commitment to the miracle of nuclear power. Nuclear energy has a mystique that generates ferocious loyalty on the part of people in the business.

Public criticism or skepticism is frequently treated just as a public relations problem. Citizens are not credited with having any legitimate input to make in the decision-making process. We are usually dismissed, as not understanding enough about the technology. We are told to trust the experts.

But we know that no technology is infallible. Three Mile Island and Chernobyl—not to mention the space shuttle Challenger tragedy—have taught us that. We should be able to raise questions and express reservations, without being patronized or ridiculed.

Concern ourselves

The safety of nuclear power reactors is a perfectly legitimate concern. For me, the wastes from uranium mines, refineries and nuclear plants are an even greater scandal. How dare we as a society dig up uranium and build nuclear plants, for 40 years now, when we still do not know how to handle the lethal garbage that results? What if we can *never* find an adequately safe method? We will have dumped a massive problem on the environment, leaving it for future generations to handle. That strikes me as the ultimate in irresponsibility. It takes some pretty fancy footwork to argue that that is not ethically reprehensible.

What can we do against the strength of the nuclear lobby? Some Canadian churches have adopted policies calling for a moratorium on any further expansion of uranium mining and nuclear power until some of these problems can be solved. Churches in Saskatchewan have gone on record as wanting uranium mining completely halted in their province. They are concerned not only about the environmental problems, but also about the possible use of Saskatchewan uranium by other countries to manufacture nuclear bombs.

Support groups against nuclear power

Environmental groups throughout Canada have called for the complete phasing out of nuclear power. Energy Probe and the Canadian Coalition for Nuclear Responsibility have probably done the most in researching the problems related to nuclear power. Both groups have tried to organize resistance to an increasing dependence in Canada, particularly Ontario, on nuclear-generated power. In Saskatchewan, the Inter-Church Uranium Committee has spent years in patient research and education about the problems related to uranium mining. Citizen groups in the Maritimes opposed the building of the reactor at Point LePreau, New Brunswick. I am sure that they will respond again if the building of LePreau II becomes more than a rumor.

Supporting the efforts of groups like these can help expand the base of concerned citizens.

Our politicians have to accept more responsibility for decisions related to nuclear power. A lot of the shots are presently called by the crown corporations involved in uranium mining and nuclear power. These include Cameco in Saskatchewan (which is to be gradually privatized), Ontario Hydro, and Atomic Energy of Canada Ltd. These corporations often seem to function like independent states. But they are largely financed with public funds. We need to press our elected officials to change the system so that crown corporations are more open to public scrutiny.

Use less energy

One last word. The nuclear industry paints a bleak scenario of our society, were we to phase out nuclear power. They promise massive energy shortages that would cripple our economy; they claim we would have to switch to coal-generated power, thus drastically increasing our acid rain and greenhouse problems. But there are other scenarios.

Canada could dramatically reduce its energy consumption. Already, many technological innovations would allow our society to run on less power. If significant research money were allocated, much more could be done. These options are not encouraged in part because powerful energy-producing sectors in our society have a vested interest in keeping us gobbling up massive amounts of energy.

A study done for the federal Dept. of Energy, Mines and Resources, by the environmental group Friends of the Earth, detailed the technical and economic feasibility of Canada using much less energy—without any significant negative impact on our standard of living.

Energy conservation and efficiency could be Canada's single greatest source of energy. We need not be captive to nuclear power.

Resources for further information

Energy Probe, 100 College St., Toronto, ON, M5G 1L5 (416)978-7014

Canadian Coalition for Nuclear Responsibility, C.P. 236, Succursale Snowdon, Montreal, P.Q. H3X 3T4

The Inter-Church Uranium Committee, Box 7724, Saskatoon, SK, S7K 4R4 (306) 934-3030

High up in the sky the ozone layer surrounds the earth, protecting us from dangerous ultraviolet rays. Now we are destroying it too.

Ozone Layer
Killing the heavens

We humans seem no longer content with destroying the earth with our pollution. Now we are killing the heavens too.

The ozone layer sounds like some technical term from a science fiction movie. An increasing number of people know better. We are learning that it is a layer of gas in the upper atmosphere. We are also becoming aware that something serious is happening to it, something that could have profound effects on human health. And it is pretty clear now that this change comes not from natural causes but as a direct result of our chemical lifestyle.

Ozone is a pungent-smelling gas, closely related to oxygen. Most of us have smelled ozone briefly after a thunderstorm. That strange, delightfully fresh odor comes from the lightning splitting ordinary oxygen molecules, which reform as ozone.

The vast majority of the earth's ozone exists far above the earth's surface. A layer of ozone about 20 km thick surrounds the earth in the upper atmosphere, the stratosphere. This layer starts around 15 km above the earth's surface, about 5 km higher than most planes fly.

Depleting our only shield

Scientists have discovered that the ozone layer plays a critical role in maintaining life on the planet. The ozone absorbs much of the dangerous ultraviolet rays coming from the sun. Among humans, those rays can cause skin cancer, damage the eyes and suppress the body's immune system, leaving it more vulnerable to disease. Research indicates that as little as a 1% reduction in the ozone layer could result in a 4% increase in skin cancer. Increased ultraviolet rays could also reduce growth of some of the world's most important crops. Aquatic life living near the ocean's surface is also vulnerable. Damage to the ozone layer could have a major impact on fish populations. In fact, any significant damage to the ozone layer that allowed more ultraviolet rays to reach the earth would have a major effect on virtually every life form.

Over the past ten years, monitoring of the stratosphere has revealed a worrisome development. The ozone layer seems to be slowly depleting. Over Canada, it has been reduced by 3-5% since 1975. But the really shocking news was the discovery of a "hole" in the ozone layer over Antarctica. During the springtime, an area of the ozone layer about the size of the United States becomes exceedingly thin, reduced by about 40%. Environment Canada scientists have recently detected a possible similar "hole" above the Arctic. That's getting pretty close to home.

Causes of ozone depletion

Ozone is very fragile. It can easily be affected by other chemicals. Pollution from the earth has been slowly drifting into the upper atmosphere. Some types of chemical pollutants react with the ozone, gradually destroying it.

The principal culprits are CFCs, chlorofluorocarbons, sometimes called freon gases. These gases do not appear in nature. They are totally the product of human engineering. They were developed for a variety of industrial and consumer uses—such as propellants in aerosol spray cans. They are also employed in manufacturing foam insulation and padding, as coolants in refrigerators and air-conditioners, and in some cleaning solvents.

CFCs were originally considered quite safe. They were not toxic, non-flammable and did not seem to have any negative environmental effects. In fact, CFCs were considered a break-through invention, and replaced other chemicals which were suspected of being much more dangerous to human health.

We are seeing this pattern more and more as society becomes increasingly complex. A solution to one problem turns out later to have effects more serious than the problem it was intended to overcome. I can understand why some people despair about the future of our civilization.

The oversight in the testing of CFCs was that researchers only looked at the lower atmosphere. In the lower atmosphere, CFCs appear to be very stable. But when they reach the upper atmosphere, they break down. One of the resulting products is chlorine. Chlorine is an extremely active chemical—and an absolute killer when it comes to ozone. As the chlorine interacts with ozone, ozone molecules are destroyed, setting up a chain reaction. One chlorine atom can lead to the destruction of a hundred thousand ozone molecules.

Thousands of tonnes of CFCs from various uses were dumped into the atmosphere during the 1970s. They started chemical changes in the upper atmosphere, and the ozone layer started dying. As far as we know, the ozone layer had existed unaltered for millions of years since the early days of the earth's existence. Now, within less than a decade, we see it being destroyed. We are a frighteningly powerful species in our destructive capacity.

Not only is it taking us so little time to start wreaking havoc with the upper atmosphere, but it will take a long time to undo our damage—if it can be undone. CFCs can survive in the atmosphere for over 75 years. Because CFCs are a relatively recent invention, all the CFCs that have ever been released into the atmosphere are still there. Even if we totally stopped all further release of CFCs, today, our ozone layer would continue to be eaten away for at least three generations. Yet at current rates, about 800,000 to one million tonnes of CFCs are *added* each year to the accumulation already up there.

I visited a church recently where they told a children's story as part of the service. As I looked at the kids—their faces aglow with the carefree joy of life—I realized that because of our destruction of the ozone layer, more of them will get cancer than my generation. That hit home. Statistics about ozone depletion and cancer rates could never be so personal. The ethical concept of our responsibility to future generations became much less abstract for me at that point.

Many of us first learned of the ozone problem when we realized that the foam cups from which we drank our coffee at innumerable meetings had been manufactured with CFCs. People quickly started abandoning the foam cup in favor of reusable mugs or paper cups. Industry recognized that they had better do something. They found a way to produce foam cups without using CFCs; that is what is available in Canada now.

The same thing happened with aerosols. In the mid-1970s, the problems caused by CFCs were well enough documented to force industry in Canada to agree to reduce by 50% the use of CFCs as propellants in aerosol spray cans. The power of

Consumer pressure led industry to find a way of producing foam cups without using CFCs. Collectively we can make changes.

public pressure became apparent. People started boycotting aerosol sprays. This caused such a reduction that the 50% target was surpassed. In 1980, the Canadian government prohibited the further use of CFCs as a propellant in hair sprays, antiperspirants and deodorants. This resulted in an 86% reduction in the total use of CFCs in spray cans and a 45% overall total reduction of CFC use in Canada. Similar actions were taken in the U.S. and Europe.

In North America, spray cans are no longer the major villains. Other propellants, which *appear* not to have negative environmental effects, have replaced the CFCs. (It is possible, however, that these alternate gases may contribute to global warming.) CFCs were still allowed in other spray cans including room deodorizers, furniture polish, and spray waxes for cars. Fortunately, the aerosol industry recognized that they were contributing to a serious environmental problem. They responded to pressure from environmental groups, government, and the public, and took steps to phase out CFCs almost completely as propellants. By the end of 1988, CFCs were no longer in use in the majority of aerosol cans manufactured in Canada. The only exception is in some specialized medical uses for which there is presently no alternative.

I wish that that were the end of the story. But it appears that we have not yet learned our lesson. Use of CFCs is increasing again.

In other parts of the world, CFCs are still used in spray cans. About 1/3 of all the CFCs used in the world today are still sprayed from cans, even with virtually none of that coming from North America. The global production of CFCs is on a steady increase.

In North America, *other* industrial and consumer uses of CFCs have increased so much that production of chlorofluorocarbons is now back to the levels it had reached in the early 1970s. Foam packaging is one of those uses. Here too public pressure is having some impact. One of the most visible forms of CFC-blown foams was the egg cartons and food trays on which meat and some fruit and vegetables were packaged in grocery stores. The fast food outlets used the same kinds of foams. As people became aware of the problem with the ozone layer, supermarkets and fast food outlets started feeling the heat from environmentally-conscious consumers. By the end of 1988, such food packaging in Canada was no longer made with CFCs. People can make a difference when they express their concerns.

CFCs are still in use in foams used for other purposes, like container packaging and insulation.

One of the biggest sources of CFC emissions is automobile air-conditioners. Ironically, as the global warming trend caused by the greenhouse effect increases, more and more people will want air-conditioning in their cars to cope with the hot summers. And a lot more CFCs will be released to the atmosphere from car air-conditioners if present manufacturing, servicing and disposal practices continue. CFCs leak from these air-conditioners when they are manufactured, installed, serviced and disposed. Some leak during usage.

Home air-conditioners and large-scale models for commercial or industrial buildings are also a source of CFC emissions. Most of the gases escape during servicing and disposal.

A CFC gas is also used in most refrigerators and freezers. If an old unit is just sent to the dump, the gas will inevitably escape, and contribute to the accumulating mass of CFCs in the atmosphere.

Solvents account for almost a quarter of the total CFC emissions. The electronics industry and dry cleaners depend on a number of types of CFCs as cleaning agents. Some paint formulations use CFCs.

Chlorofluorocarbons are so integrated into our industrial and consumer lifestyles that they would seem impossible to get rid of. Meanwhile, their destructive power continues to eat away at that fragile ozone layer which protects life forms on this planet.

Is there any hope? It depends on how determined we are to do something about the problem. We humans created chloro-fluorocarbons. Only we can resolve the destruction that they cause.

What can be done

Impose stricter standards

We do know ways of handling CFCs that would result in less leakage. CFCs are sealed into refrigerators and air conditioners, but they can seep out during filling, servicing or disposal.

Stricter standards to prevent leakage could be implemented if manufacturers and consumers were willing to pay a slightly higher price for improved design and parts. CFCs could also be removed from discarded cooling systems. That is not happening now; that kind of recycling is not considered "economical."

In the production of soft foam padding, and the rigid foam that is used in packaging and home insulation, CFCs are used as a gas to "blow" the foam. During this manufacturing process, great quantities of CFCs escape into the atmosphere. This problem is getting worse. Foam insulation is becoming more popular as a building material. And in our consumer-oriented, disposable society, foam as a packaging material is increasingly prevalent.

With more effort, most of the CFCs used in foam production could be recaptured. That too is not happening very much now, because it would increase production costs. One of the most enduring values of our society seems to be, keep the costs down so that we can keep the profits up. The protection of the environment has yet to achieve comparable status as a guiding principle.

Substitute safer chemicals

Should CFCs be used at all? There is really no justification anymore for the use of CFCs in spray cans, now that other apparently safer chemicals have been developed as propellants. Do we need all the foam used in packaging?

Other existing chemicals can substitute for many of the uses of CFCs, without posing a threat to the ozone layer. Fluorocarbons can perform some of the same functions as chlorofluorocarbons, but their lack of chlorine makes them safer. Further research could undoubtedly come up with other safer chemicals which could be substituted for CFCs.

Ban CFCs

Why don't we ban CFCs completely? Or why not impose such strict regulations that manufacturers would be forced to adopt improved handling techniques and increase their use of alternate substances? I think that we are still wedded to a belief that all of our decisions as a society need to contribute to further economic growth. We reject anything that conflicts with that goal. We tolerate decisions based on other values, like social or environmental improvement, only as long as they do not cost too much money.

I have always found it strange that industries boast about their creativity and innovativeness on problems related to expanding economic growth, but appear stymied when tackling other types of problems. On almost any environmental or social issue, industry claims that stricter standards would make them less competitive, would lose business and might even cause loss of jobs.

Despite this dual personality, we have seen time and time again that environmental protection and a healthy economic lifestyle can be compatible. North America's economy did not collapse when CFCs were banned from aerosol spray cans, or when phosphates were removed from laundry detergents. But both took threats of regulation, a consumer boycott and eventual legislation before their producers yielded.

During the last year or so, I am glad to report, industry has been picking up on the ozone layer problem. Alternate manufacturing processes have been developed, in which CFCs are not used at all. As of the end of 1988, virtually all aerosol cans and foam food packaging material in Canada no longer used CFCs. The accumulating scientific evidence, the clearly evident public concern, and pressure from governments led a variety of companies to take steps to reduce the destruction of the ozone layer.

In November 1988, I attended a conference jointly sponsored by Friends of the Earth and Environment Canada. The event brought industry people together with scientists, environmentalists and government officials to talk about reducing CFC use. Initially, the industry people were very nervous about such a conference. By the end of the day, they were glad that they had come. There was good information shared, and a clear sense of people from various backgrounds working together to find solutions to an environmental crisis.

During the conference, the organizers announced three awards. One went to a government official, who had done much of the international negotiating for Canada and had provided real leadership.

A second went to a representative of industry, to acknowledge the way some companies had acted before government regulations forced them into it.

The third award, they wanted to present to the "Canadian public," recognizing how concerned people had put pressure on government and industry to do something about the ozone layer. To my surprise, they asked The United Church of Canada to accept this award on behalf of the Canadian people. They felt that the churches symbolized mainstream Canadians. In pushing for action on this issue, the churches spoke like many other citizens: we have to do something to protect this fragile earth of ours.

The ozone layer is not doomed, if we can act decisively and quickly. We have to push for much stronger controls over how CFCs are used in Canada, and internationally, and advocate the eventual elimination of them completely.

What we can do

As with many other environmental problems, threats to the ozone layer are not limited by national borders. This is truly an issue for international attention.

Canada has taken some international leadership in this area. In 1985, Canada signed the Vienna Convention for the Protection of the Ozone Layer, developed under the United Nations Environmental Program. Canada was the first nation to formally ratify that convention in June 1986. The Convention was a starting point.

Another step toward international regulation of CFCs took place in Montreal, in September 1987. Canada hosted a United Nations sponsored meeting where many nations discussed restrictions on the production and use of CFCs. The conference was hailed as a great success, because agreement was reached to reduce CFC production by 50% by 1998. However, six months after the Montreal Convention was signed, new evidence from NASA scientists indicated that the ozone layer was being destroyed even faster than had been thought. A much greater reduction than the Montreal agreement would be needed.

Support efforts to save the ozone layer

The environmental group, Friends of the Earth, has been doing a lot of research, education and lobbying about the depleting ozone layer. They recommend the virtual elimination of all production and use of CFCs. The Canadian government and several provincial governments have recently indicated that they may be prepared to agree. We can support the efforts of Friends of the Earth, by writing to the Prime Minister, the Minister of the Environment, and our Member of Parliament registering strong support for much more aggressive steps to save the ozone layer.

More research and active regulation must follow. Internationally, Canada is pushing for a long-term strategy that would reduce both the production and the release of CFCs, and control other chemicals that affect the ozone layer. This work deserves our strong support. Let our politicians know that we consider these negotiations to be essential and also urgent.

There have been some encouraging signs around the world. The European Community indicated recently that they support the goal of eliminating CFC use. Several politicians—in particular Britain's Margaret Thatcher—have been championing the cause of ozone protection.

But what they have done so far is the easy part. Working out the details of how reduction and elimination of CFC use will happen could run into many obstacles. We have to keep up the pressure.

Environmental protection must become such an overwhelming public preoccupation that governments and industries, out of their own interests for self-preservation if nothing else, will devote the necessary resources to solving environmental problems. Regulations imposed by governments should be among the most popular actions they can take. To get to that point will require a lot more public education and willingness on the part of all of us to make our concerns known.

Take responsibility as individuals

As individuals, we can do a variety of things to save the ozone layer:

a) You probably won't run into any foam coffee cups in Canada that are made with CFCs, but you might if you travel. Ask your hosts if they know about the ozone problem. Start a little international incident if you find them unaware or uncaring. However, even if Canadian foam cups aren't made with CFCs, they could still contribute to our waste disposal problem. We have to get out of our habit of using something once, then throwing it away. Why not try some old fashioned cups and saucers, and then recruit a couple of volunteers to help wash them after you're finished?

b) if you have air-conditioning in your car, check with your garage to make sure that they have equipment for trapping the CFC gases when they do the servicing. If they don't, make a fuss, particularly if it is a large dealership. Car servicing places are not likely to get the equipment that they need to trap gases unless their customers start complaining or threatening to take their business elsewhere.

c) if you are getting rid of a refrigerator or air-conditioner, make sure that it doesn't go to the dump with its gases still inside. It may take some research and pressure to find a place that will drain the gas so that it does not escape into the atmosphere. Pester your provincial Ministry of the Environment or your municipality if you have trouble disposing of the gases safely. Irate citizens help move politicians and government bureaucrats.

God created the heavens. We continue to destroy them. Changing our lifestyle so that we stop being so destructive would be a sign of respect and reverence for this creation.

Resources for further information

Ozone Campaign Kit, Friends of the Earth, Suite 701, 251 Laurier Ave.W., Ottawa, ON, K1P 5J6, (613) 230-3352

If the greenhouse effect is not dealt with now, we could see good agricultural land, such as Canada's prairies, become desert.

Greenhouse Effect
An overheated world

About eighty of us gathered in a downtown Washington hotel. The director of a centre in India that works on peace, justice and environmental issues sat next to an agricultural worker from Bolivia. One of the world's leading climatologists from England sat near a rural minister from Fiji. An American land use planner was with a consumer activist from Malaysia. On my left was a Swiss minister concerned about ecology, on my right a representative of the Kenyan Ministry of the Environment.

We had gathered from around the world to establish a network of non-governmental organizations, to pressure governments for action on a phenomenon that humanity is only just starting to learn about, but which may dramatically affect the lives of everyone on earth—the greenhouse effect.

In earlier chapters of this book, I looked at the problems of acid rain, toxic wastes, nuclear wastes and reduction of the ozone layer. These are all serious issues and need to be solved. The greenhouse effect may have more dramatic impact on human civilization than any of the others.

What makes the greenhouse effect so significant is that it affects the climate around the world. In fact, it is *already* affecting the earth's climate. Since the beginning of this century, the earth's average temperatures have risen between 0.3 and 1.1 degrees celsius as a direct result of increased greenhouse gases in the atmosphere.

And the increase appears to be accelerating as the century progresses. Though they cannot say for sure, many scientists think it is no coincidence that five of the hottest years this century have occurred in the 1980s!

One of the first discoveries, when talking about the greenhouse effect, is how much we *don't* know. Climatic change is massive in scope; many variables affect it. Just think how frequently the weather report is wrong about tomorrow's weather! Imagine how much more difficult it is to project 50 or 100 years down the road, taking into account not only natural dynamics but changes caused by human societies.

As with many other environmental issues, an incredible amount of research needs to be done. That takes money and trained people. We have the money—if we decide that the future of the earth matters enough to channel our resources into the needed research. As for the trained personnel, we have to pray that young people have not become so cynical about the future—because of society's past and present behavior—that they turn away from careers that will help preserve the earth. The greenhouse effect will need many bright young minds studying the problem and developing solutions.

Scientists have been able to discover some of what is happening. They know that the earth is going through a gradual warming of its atmosphere. There have been highs and lows during the past century but on average our climate *is* warming. The apparent cause is the increase in gases from human sources in the atmosphere. Radiation from the sun penetrates through these gases to the earth. In earlier centuries, much of the heat used to reflect off of the earth and go back out through the atmosphere. The gases now accumulating in the atmosphere absorb these rays, and prevent them from escaping back out into space. This layer of pollution gases acts like a massive blanket around the globe, causing the earth's surface to grow steadily warmer.

This trend will likely accelerate, unless we reduce the amount of polluting gas we pump into the atmosphere.

Causes of the greenhouse effect

The major culprit contributing to the greenhouse effect is carbon dioxide (CO_2). Carbon dioxide is a naturally occurring element in the atmosphere. It has always been there. Scientists, tracing the amounts of carbon dioxide in the atmosphere, have related CO_2 levels to the ice age. Heavy glaciation happened when there was a low level of CO_2 in the atmosphere. The technical measurement is *parts per million by volume* or ppmv. During the ice age it was about 200 ppmv; during warm periods it was around 275 ppmv.

Scientists know that there was a correlation between CO_2 levels and the ice ages or warm periods. They cannot say which one caused the other. Still, there was not much variation. Over more than a thousand *centuries*, carbon dioxide concentrations in the atmosphere have fluctuated between 200 and 275 ppmv.

Just before the industrial revolution, the CO_2 levels stood at around 275 ppmv. Since then, they have increased steadily. Today, they stand at 345 ppmv. In less than 200 years, the *increase* in carbon dioxide in the atmosphere has been as great as the entire range of CO_2 levels over the previous 150,000 years.

The major source of this new carbon dioxide has been our burning of fossil fuels like coal, oil and gas, to produce energy. Sound familiar? Carbon dioxide coming from coal-burning electrical generating plants is a prime source of acid rain. CO_2 from the same sources contributes to the greenhouse effect. Most of this carbon dioxide comes from the energy hungry industrialized countries of North America, Europe and Japan. Worldwide, about 5 billion tonnes of CO_2 are emitted annually into the atmosphere.

Carbon dioxide is the biggest contributing factor to the greenhouse effect. It makes up about 50% of the greenhouse gases. But it is not the only gas that we have to worry about. Other gases from our human activity also accumulate in the atmosphere and contribute to the greenhouse effect.

Chlorofluorocarbons, or CFCs, which are devastating the ozone layer, also play a supporting role in the greenhouse effect drama. At present, there is a much smaller quantity of CFCs in the atmosphere than carbon dioxide. CFCs constitute about 10% of the greenhouse gases. However, each molecule of a chlorofluorocarbon is 10,000 times more powerful as a "heat blanket" than a molecule of carbon dioxide. And we only started pumping them into the atmosphere two decades ago!

In addition to carbon dioxide and CFCs, several other gases have been identified as major contributors to the greenhouse effect. Methane, emitted from natural gas and from some rotting organic matter, contributes about 20%. Nitrous oxide which comes from fertilizers and the burning of coal, oil and gas makes up around 10%.

Researchers are experimenting with computer models, to project how much the earth's temperature will increase as these gases accumulate. They are very cautious, because there are so many unknowns. One benchmark used to calculate trends is a doubling of the pre-industrial level of CO_2 in the atmosphere. What happens if the carbon dioxide level increases from the 275 ppmv of 1800 to 550 ppmv?

That doubling point could be reached as early as 2050. And it would probably lead to an increase in the earth's temperature of anywhere from 1.5 to 4.5 degrees celsius. This may not seem like much. But it would be enough to melt the polar ice caps, flooding many coastal regions. Vast areas of the earth would become desert, including Canada's prairies. Catastrophic storms would increase in frequency and intensity. A little rise in the earth's temperature can do a lot of damage.

The highly industrialized countries of the developed world—North America, Europe and Japan—are by far the biggest per capita emitters of carbon dioxide. We not only

A small rise in the earth's temperature would be enough to melt massive glaciers and polar ice caps, flooding many coastal regions.

gobble up a disproportionate share of the world's energy resources, but we also pollute the atmosphere—with gases created as we burn this coal, oil and gas—far out of proportion to our population.

At the same time, human activity has rapidly been destroying one of nature's natural buffers against CO_2 buildup. The world's tropical rain forests, located primarily in developing countries, are being cut down at an alarming rate. As the rain forests disappear, the greenhouse effect becomes more serious. Trees and plant life in general act as something of a filtration system for the earth's atmosphere. They absorb carbon dioxide and release oxygen as part of their process of growth.

Some of these forests are being cut to feed the world's voracious appetite for lumber. The lands being logged are inadequately reforested. In other areas, the rain forests are cut and burned to provide land for grazing cattle. Large beef ranches are replacing Central and South American rain forests; much of the meat makes hamburgers for North Americans. Peasants trying to find some land to raise a few crops cut down forests as well. Because the soil is rarely good for farming, after a couple of years they have to move on to another tract of forest, where the cycle starts over again.

The rain forests around the world were once so massive that they could absorb a great deal of the carbon dioxide emitted into the atmosphere. Now, as they are being destroyed, this buffer capacity diminishes. As we produce increasing amounts of carbon dioxide and other greenhouse gases, the capacity of nature to absorb them declines. It's a double whammy.

You will likely hear people blaming Brazil and other countries for contributing to the greenhouse effect by cutting their rain forests. Such righteous indignation is rather misplaced. We in the northern industrial countries are the primary creators of the pollution that is affecting the atmosphere. If the rain forests are not going to be around, we can hardly blame those countries for not cleaning up *our* garbage. The real source of the problem lies in our own backyard.

I predict that environmental problems will be one of the primary causes of international tensions in the next few decades. Brazil, and a number of other developing countries, recently told the world that only they would decide what happens to their rain forests. They resent industrialized countries lecturing them about the global environment.

And I don't point the finger only at capitalist countries. We are not the only offenders; the whole industrialized world is. The U.S.S.R. and the Eastern European countries are just beginning to wake up to the seriousness of their environmental record. In terms of the capacity to pollute, we share much more with those countries than we do with the southern developing nations. A great deal of the industrial development of Eastern Europe and the U.S.S.R. depends on energy created by burning of fossil fuels—coal, oil and gas. They are thus major contributors to the production of greenhouse gases. Their economies are not particularly strong these days so they may find it even more difficult to make some of the changes than we will.

China is not yet one of the heavily industrialized nations. But dramatic economic developments are occurring in the world's most populous country. The leadership and the people of China seem intent on making major strides. But one of their principal sources of energy, to propel this economic giant, is the most problematic of the fossil fuels: coal. Burning coal is the major source of carbon dioxide emissions worldwide. China has vast reserves of coal. Who can blame them for planning to use this natural resource to generate the energy that they will need?

I can imagine the reaction of a country like China if we were to call on it to limit its use of coal. We in the industrialized countries, whose economies are already well established, created the greenhouse problem. Then we ask a country, just embarking on a major expansion, to limit its development because of our mistakes? That would not sit too well.

How such environmental problems get worked out on an international scale will be one of the major challenges for global relations in the next few decades. The potential for international co-operation is tremendous. The price of failure will be disastrous.

Impacts of the greenhouse effect

Scientists again profess their ignorance when it comes to forecasting exactly the effects of a global warming. There are, however, a number of distinct possibilities that they cite:
• significant melting of ice at poles
• sea levels rising between 1 and 5 feet
• low-lying countries flooding
• violent storms increasing in maritime areas
• some interior areas becoming much drier
• good agricultural land turning to desert
• severe droughts occurring more frequently
Environment Canada's recent studies project billions of dollars of losses in agricultural production on the prairies and in Ontario. Much of the prairies could be an annual dustbowl.

The water level of the Great Lakes would fall because of less rain and snow. Shipping costs would increase by about 30%. Many recreation areas along the Lakes would vanish. Hydro power, which relies on heavy water flow, would be reduced.

On Canada's maritime coasts, rising sea levels and storm tides could cause billions of dollars in damage and reconstruction expenses. Industries, residences, farmland, sewage systems, railways and highways in low-lying coastal areas could all be threatened. Much of the Fraser Valley in B.C. and the Annapolis Valley in Nova Scotia would be under water.

Almost everyone in Canada would be affected dramatically by these kinds of changes. When we bring it down to the level of our own situation, global pollution starts to look less remote. Losing a farm to drought, a house to a rising sea level, a cottage to a dried-up lake, makes the greenhouse effect a lot more personal.

The global warming may make northern areas more suitable for farming than at present. Some people grasp at this straw of potential agricultural benefits from the greenhouse effect, as a way of downplaying the need for action. That is a pretty weak straw. As scientists are the first to acknowledge, there is much uncertainty about the effects of major climatic change. It is a risky game to gamble that our polluting lifestyle will have net beneficial results. The stakes are the lives and economies of entire regions and countries.

At that Washington meeting, it became very clear that the effects might be felt more disastrously in some regions of the world than in others. In many poorer nations, like India, Bangladesh and much of Southeast Asia, a large percentage of the population lives in coastal regions, on land within a few metres of sea level. If the seas rise, huge areas of these countries will be under water. Some island nations could disappear completely.

African nations are already in a crisis, with the severe droughts of recent years causing the starvation of millions of people. Some scientists believe that there is a connection between these droughts and the early stages of the greenhouse effect. If that is the case, the future of some African countries is pretty bleak.

Several times during the Washington meeting, the anxiety and anger of representatives of these countries erupted. They found themselves once again victims of the economic lifestyles of the richer part of the world. They found it offensive, that they were being invited to share in the *sacrifices* and costs of dealing with the greenhouse effect, without having benefitted from the industrial development that had created the problem in the first place.

Developing nations are imprisoned by the horrendous

debts that they owe to western governments and banks. Each year, billions of dollars in interest payments flow from their economies to ours. They have little chance of meeting the basic needs of their people, let alone tackling global environmental problems. The Third World participants at the Washington meeting resented talks about global action while their need for relief from these debts went unrecognized.

Many of these developing countries are tackling population growth, recognizing that such growth places a great strain on their resources and requires them to produce more energy, leading to more greenhouse gases. But it is still our industrialized countries that use by far the most energy resources in the world, even with our smaller populations.

The Third World participants had many reasons to be frustrated with those of us from industrialized countries. But they did not walk out of the meeting. They realized we are all in this together. With more generosity than we have shown them in the past, they indicated their willingness to be a part of the search for solutions.

I want to pause for a brief editorial comment. I talked about the greenhouse effect as mainly caused by the industrial, energy-hungry processes of our modern lifestyle. Canada and other highly industrialized countries are the main contributors to the problem. As with other pollution, we are creating a lot of problems, but many others around the world have to share the consequences.

I do not write this to make you feel guilty. I would be undermining my purpose in writing this book if I simply immobilized you with guilt.

In describing the problems from local garbage to the global greenhouse effect, I want to provide *information* about the sources of our difficulties *so that we can plan effective change.*

I have tried, as accurately as possible, to describe the serious environmental problems that I see before us. You may disagree with some aspects of my analysis, but I do not think that *anyone* can argue against the fact that our mistakes are now catching up with us. To do something about them, we must understand them. That is what this book is about.

Guilt will not get us out of our difficulties. Understanding the problems and committing ourselves to doing something about them will.

What we can do

We can not control the weather. But we can control some factors that affect the weather.

We are not used to thinking on such a grand scale. But the way in which the atmospheric warming could influence the weather, and the impact of such changes in weather, are new and dramatic developments in the history of our planet. Human activity caused this warming; human activity could turn it around.

Reject nuclear power

Carbon dioxide is our biggest problem. Much of it comes from power plants using fossil fuels, primarily coal. There are two main ways to use less coal: increase our use of nuclear power, or put much more emphasis on energy efficiency and conservation. The first choice continues our present extravagant ways; the second reduces the amount of energy that needs to be generated.

Building large numbers of nuclear plants will not do much to minimize the greenhouse effect. Even to reduce by half the world fossil fuel use, there would need to be thirteen nuclear plants completed *each week for 25 years!* Not only is such a construction schedule physically impossible, but 25 years would be too late to avert some major effects of the global warming.

Secondly, switching to nuclear power introduces a whole series of other environmental problems—ranging from uranium mining, through to nuclear plant safety and what to

do with the high-level radioactive wastes. We have recently
learned of the scandalous history of safety and environmental
violations from plants related to the U.S. nuclear arms program. There will almost certainly be more serious problems
in the future, as nuclear power plants grow older. Three Mile
Island and Chernobyl could be just the beginning.

Thirdly, it would be prohibitively expensive to build the
necessary number of nuclear plants. The construction would
require massive amounts of public spending. Some estimates
put it at almost $2 trillion to switch from fossil fuels to
nuclear power in the United States. That is more than ten
times the size of the present annual U.S. federal deficit.

Such large expenditures on nuclear plants would actually
add to the problem. There would be less money available for
the more effective strategies to combat global warming—
increased conservation and energy efficiency.

And finally, a resort to nuclear power perpetuates the
mentality that we constantly need more energy, without
pushing us to search for more long-term, sustainable ways of
functioning as a society.

Improve energy efficiency and conservation

There is another way if we have the imagination and
commitment to pursue it. Increasing the efficiency with which
our societies use energy is the most effective, fastest, and
most economical way to reduce our dependence on energy
produced by the burning of fossil fuels.

We already have some of the technology available to
significantly improve the energy efficiency of many of our
household and industrial uses. Newly developed lightbulbs
use a fraction of the electricity needed by the ordinary kind.
Refrigerators, air-conditioners and other household appliances can be built which require much less energy. Industries
can use their own wastes to generate the power they need.

To reduce the amount of electricity now produced by
American coal-fired plants by half, through improved energy

efficiency, would require an investment of about 2.7 cents per kilowatt-hour. To create new nuclear plants to replace the same amount of coal-fired power would cost between 10 and 15 cents per kilowatt-hour.

Improved energy efficiency and conservation can make the difference we need to reduce our fossil fuel use. We can help reduce the global warming trend significantly through such approaches. And what's more, we can each make a difference at an individual level.

The possibilities become even more hopeful when you add the potential of new renewable energy sources. Many people are skeptical about renewable energy sources like solar, small hydroelectric plants, wind turbines and others. In the past, these technologies have had little chance to prove themselves. Compare the amount of research and development money that has gone into nuclear power with research into renewable energy sources, and you'll understand why renewable sources have been slower getting off the ground. In Canada, we have pumped billions of dollars, our public taxes, into the nuclear industry because many of the major companies are crown corporations like Atomic Energy of Canada Limited (AECL), Ontario Hydro and (until recently) Eldorado Nuclear. Yet every time the federal government starts budget-cutting, the first targets are the already minimal funds going into programs related to conservation and renewable energy.

Our federal government hosted a major international conference on the greenhouse effect in June 1988. The Prime Minister told participants that Canada eagerly awaited the conference's recommendations. Yet within two months, the federal cabinet had cut funding for energy conservation and renewable energy development. It reduced the staff by 50%. Between 1984 and 1988, the federal government cut funding for these programs by 81%.

Yet, these are precisely the kinds of programs we need to help solve the greenhouse effect.

Conservation, energy efficiency and new renewable energy

sources can make a big difference to the global warming trend. These are not just pipe dreams. A study done in the late 1970s for the federal Department of Energy, Mines and Resources documented in specific and practical terms how Canada could use much less energy, while still maintaining a high standard of living.

But politicians have not gotten the message—the message that we care about how we use energy resources. I guess we have not been too clear about it ourselves. The greenhouse effect brings the matter into focus dramatically. By making our opinions felt forcefully, Canada, one of the world's biggest per capita energy users, can provide a more responsible example.

At the same time, there are many ways that we can reduce our own energy use: ensuring that our home is adequately insulated, limiting unnecessary use of electrical appliances, reducing our use of cars, using more public transit or our bicycles or walking legs. Energy conservation begins at home.

As we learn more about the greenhouse effect, we have to put a lot more resources into research and solving the problem before it gets completely out of hand. Life on this planet depends on us taking assertive action.

Resources for further information

Friends of the Earth Kit on the Greenhouse Effect, available from Friends of the Earth, Suite 701, 251 Laurier Ave. W., Ottawa, ON, K1P 5J6, (613) 230-3352

Turning Down the Heat: Solutions to Global Warming, Public Citizens' Critical Mass Energy Project, 215 Pennsylvania Ave. SE, Washington, D.C., 20003, (202) 546-4996 (U.S.$20)

Understanding CO_2 and Climate, Environment Canada, Canadian Climate Centre, Atmospheric Environment Service, 4905 Dufferin St., Toronto, ON, M3H 5T4

*Third World countries need economic development, but can we help
them without causing more destructive environmental side-effects?*

Third World
How Canada helps destroy the global environment

We usually think that "development" refers to projects
helping poor and undernourished people in the Third World.
Sometimes it does. But there is a growing awareness that
many development projects are not exclusively beneficial.
They may have a destructive effect on the environment and
on the natural resources of these countries. People who were
intended to benefit may in the long term be much worse off.

To take one example, hydroelectric power schemes meant

to provide electricity to remote areas (and to fuel industrial expansion in the urban areas) flood massive tracts of agricultural land. Thousands of people are forced to relocate to areas that are unsuitable for their traditional farming techniques. Dams end the annual flooding that brought needed nutritional silt to fertilize the river banks; huge quantities of chemical fertilizers have to be used to compensate. The quality of the soil diminishes.

In attempting to provide farm land for poor peasants, some governments have used foreign aid to build roads into uninhabited tropical forest areas. These forests, like those in the Amazon Basin, act as natural air-conditioners and air purifiers for the earth. The soil which supported the forests for centuries is thin and unsuitable for agriculture. After a couple of years of unsuccessful farming, the peasants sell the land to ranchers, who bring in cattle. The peasants move farther into the forests, and repeat the destructive cycle.

Producing more products, such as meat for export, has been one means of increasing the economic independence of developing countries. But the consequences of some of these projects prove disastrous. Vast areas of land which once supported forests or family farms are taken over for huge cattle ranches. Cattle trample the ground, compact the earth and eliminate any possibility of reforestation. More soil erosion occurs. All this contributes to the growth of the world's deserts.

"Desertification" refers to the deterioration of land until it can no longer support agricultural growth. These vast cattle ranches are one of the causes of desertification.

Even projects that do a lot of good can create major problems. An important factor contributing to increased food production is irrigation. Yet, through deficiencies in planning, mismanagement, and problems that weren't or perhaps couldn't have been foreseen, vast tracts of agricultural land may be permanently damaged through waterlogging, inadequate drainage and excessive concentrations of salt.

There are also increasing examples of pollution as poor countries industrialize. Laws and regulations regarding environmental protection are relatively new even in Canada. In much of the developing world, they hardly exist. The economic struggles in many of these countries make their governments hesitant to impose pollution control orders, for fear that the companies will move their plants elsewhere. Both public and private companies operate in ways that would not be permitted under our kinds of environmental laws.

The problems, and their political implications, become very complicated. There is a long history of distrust between developing countries and industrialized ones. When our countries started raising some questions about the potential ecological consequences of some approaches to development, poorer countries suspected that we were willing to sacrifice their economic survival in order to protect the environment. We had encouraged these countries to transplant our large-scale technologies. Then, after contributing to the problems, we wanted to pull the rug out from under them, because we felt our own interests in the global environment threatened.

Canadian foreign aid has funded many large projects that have had serious environmental side-effects. We also participate through international lending institutions like the World Bank, which have supported some massive schemes with unintended destructive consequences. Now we have a moral obligation to assume some responsibility for the results of past development projects that we have both initiated and encouraged.

Third World development problems

Discovering the side-effects of large-scale hydro dams

I'm often amazed at how our ideas of what is good for development can change so dramatically over the years. Hydro dams used to be identified as a positive contribution to improving the lives of people in the Third World. Hydro power provides electricity, considered indispensable for rescuing people from poverty and increasing their standard of living. The construction of these dams provided jobs for many. Unlike plants that use coal or oil, hydro power draws on a renewable resource—water. Hydro dams do not belch out polluting smoke. Once operating, dams can help control damaging floods and provide regulated flows of water for irrigation projects. What is more, hydroelectric developments can be located where they are needed most: over a quarter of the world's hydro potential is in Asia, one-fifth in South America, one-sixth in Africa.

But it does not work out quite that positively. A look at a couple of situations will show why.

India is a big country. It has more people than any other nation except China. Feeding its hundreds of millions of citizens is a major challenge. Providing irrigation and elec- tricity for such a population is a gigantic feat. India has made remarkable progress. Over the past 15 years, it has changed from being the largest recipient of food aid in the world, to having extra to share with needier countries.

The building of large hydro dams for power and irrigation continues, with one of the most massive hydroelectric schemes in the world. The Narmada Valley Dam Project (if completed as planned) will have 30 major dams, 135 me- dium-sized ones and more than 3000 small ones. It will take 50 years to build and will cost tens of billions of dollars. The World Bank is pushing India to proceed. Canada is a member of the World Bank.

All this progress, however, has costs that may undermine many of the gains.

The land which will be flooded by the first phase of the project has been home to over 65,000 people. They are going to have to be relocated to the hillside areas around the lake. Forests on these hills will be cut down by the peasants to clear land for growing their food. Unfortunately, the soils are not the same as those they were used to. Without the trees, the soil in these areas will not be able to withstand the rains. Much of it will erode into the lake. The people will not be able to feed themselves anymore. The build-up of silt behind the dam in the reservoir will diminish the flow of water through it and seriously reduce its usefulness.

India has already found similar problems in other areas. Research at 17 major reservoirs indicates that they are silting up three times as fast as was anticipated. The huge Tehri Dam is now expected to be usable for only 30 to 40 years rather than over 100 years as originally planned.

Brazil is also discovering the hazards of large hydro dams. They are building in rain forests, where a whole chain reaction of effects occurs.

Curua Una, one of the newer dams in the Amazon basin, is already having problems. Decomposing vegetation from the forests flooded by the dam has acidified the water, corroding the steel casings of the turbines. Water hyacinth and other weeds have grown on the new lake. The weeds are toxic for some fish. They blanket the water surface, blocking the sun's rays, killing other plants and fish in the lake. The weeds increase evaporation, reducing the amount of available water in the dam, and jeopardizing both irrigation and electrical generation.

At another dam, the Jupia on the Parana River, the weight of the water hyacinths growing on the lake's surface has caused steel cables to snap. Filters designed to protect the turbines from the weeds have become so clogged that the turbines have to be shut down regularly.

In Sri Lanka, hundreds of millions of dollars were spent building four dams, for electricity and irrigation. The dams were supposed to allow 320,000 acres of rain forest and marginal scrub lands to be exploited for agriculture. Unfortunately, only about 8% of the forests in the watershed were left standing. The hillsides had no trees to root into the soil. With over 100 inches of rainfall annually, landslides now pose a serious threat to one of the dams. Over 100,000 people live in the pathway of the flood that would result.

Large hydroelectric projects also tend to distribute their benefits and costs inequitably. Most of the power does not go to improving the quality of life in the rural areas at all. According to the World Bank, 90 to 95% of electric power investments in developing countries provides power for big cities and industry. But most of the sacrifices have to be borne by the rural people.

The shores around reservoirs often provide ideal conditions for disease. In Ghana, the percentage of people affected by a disease carried by snails increased from 5 to over 80% with the building of the Volta River dam. Diarrhea rates in Kenya have jumped 70% in areas affected by hydro dams around the Tana River.

Huge hydroelectric power projects provide benefits. But are they worth the long-term costs to the population and to the environment?

Consuming the forests

The forests of the world are threatened. The assaults come from many directions. Large multinational companies gobble huge tracts of rain forest to feed their voracious appetite for lumber. Greed and minimal governmental regulations lead them to neglect adequate reforesting. Massive destruction of rain forests also occurs from building new roads, and large projects like dams, cattle ranches, mines and cash-crop farms.

The major destroyer of tropical rain forests is the international logging industry. In Papua New Guinea, Jant, a subsidiary of the Japanese company Honshu Paper, has rights to 330 square miles of rain forest which they are systematically clear-cutting. It should be all deforested by 1990. Twenty thousand tonnes of wood are shipped monthly to the Honshu paper factory in Japan. Jant sells its wood to its parent company at such a low price that they never register a profit and thus escape paying income taxes in Papua New Guinea. The company is supposed to reforest the area as they cut. In fact, they are clearing ten times faster than they are replanting.

Some countries open up huge tracts of tropical forests to give plots of land to peasants in so-called land reform schemes.

Brazil initiated its huge Polonoreste Project in 1982 with financial assistance from The World Bank. The cost of paving Highway 364 into the area alone cost around $250 million. Each year, hundreds of thousands of people have left their homes and ventured into the State of Rondonia in search of land and a new life.

They do not find what they expected. They try farming the same ways that they did in the temperate regions from which

Rain forests are rapidly being destroyed in the name of development of one kind or another. The need for reforestation seems forgotten.

they came. But the rain forest soil is thin and cannot support their agriculture. After repeated crop failures, they are forced to abandon their dream. Some sell their land to cattle ranchers or speculators. Some move on to other areas and start the process all over again, cutting farther into the diminishing rain forests. In some of the settlement areas, as many as 80% of the migrants have sold their land and moved on after less than four years.

The peasants still lack a stable land base; the forests have been destroyed—a double loss.

As recently as 1970, the State of Rondonia had plentiful forests. Calculations now indicate that if deforestation continues at the present rate, the entire state will have lost all its forests within a few years—an area two-thirds the size of Newfoundland! In addition, many plant and animal species that depended on the rain forests will disappear.

A third problem for the world's beleaguered forests is the burning of wood for heating and cooking. Wood is the main fuel for people in most poor countries. They scavenge their area for dead branches or they cut trees. More and more trees disappear as populations increase.

Over 80% of the energy needs for heating and cooking in Africa are met by burning wood. This figure rises to 90% in the poorest countries. Until recently, wood was plentiful. But that is quickly changing.

Fuel wood is being used up much more quickly than trees can regenerate. There are already severe shortages in many Third World countries. Over 100 million people are already without sufficient wood supplies for their cooking and heating needs. The same problem threatens 1.3 billion more. An increasing amount of time each day has to be spent by people, particularly women, scrounging for wood for fuel.

Industrial pollution felt in developing countries

No one denies that the economic position of many Third World countries is precarious. They need industries to create employment and generate income. Governments have gone out of their way to avoid antagonizing multinational firms. Environmental protection and the health of the countries' citizens have been prime victims of this negligence. Companies have taken advantage of weak or non-existent pollution laws. They have ravaged both land and seas for ever greater profits. They have turned a blind eye to the people they harm.

Canada is implicated in this scandal. An example of the destruction of a fragile environment in a Third World country involves a Canadian company operating in the Philippines. Placer Development Ltd. of Vancouver owns 40% of the shares of the Marcopper Mining Corporation (another 48% were owned by former President Ferdinand Marcos, and now are controlled by the Philippine Government).

For generations, Marinduque Island was inhabited by people living in close harmony with their environment. The island was a tropical paradise, surrounded by warm seas and coral reefs. More than 80% of the residents lived off the plentiful resources of the sea. They caught a wide variety of fish including tunas, sharks, mackerels, anchovies and different coral reef fishes.

In 1969, Marcopper started extracting copper from an open pit mine on Marinduque. For the first years, they deposited the mine tailings in a pond on the island. Mine tailings—the residues left after the copper has been removed from the ore—contain ground rock, potentially harmful minerals, and chemicals used in the extraction process. Marcopper stopped using the pond in 1975 when they discovered a rich ore body beneath it. From that point on, Marcopper dumped the tailings directly into the sea. The company threw about 28,000 tonnes of tailings into the Calancan Bay every day. Over 100 million tonnes of tailing sand have poured on top of the coral on the sea floor, covering around 50 square kilometres.

After dumping of mine tailings into Calancan Bay started, the numbers and variety of fish in the fishermen's nets began to decrease. According to groups working with the residents, the fishermen catch only about 10% of what they used to, hardly enough to feed their own families let alone sell for a living. The flora and fauna of the bay have been devastated. In the area of greatest concentration of mine tailings, nothing survives. Further away, the few species still surviving are mostly immature or diseased. The livelihood of the fishermen and their families has been virtually wiped out.

At the same time, the incidence of respiratory, stomach and skin illnesses among the coastal residents has increased dramatically. Abdominal pains and diarrhea are common after the people eat fish from the area.

As if that weren't bad enough, the land also suffers. During the dry season, winds carry fine particles from the exposed tailings inland, covering agricultural lands, destroying plant life and contaminating the residents' drinking water. Respiratory illnesses are particularly high during the summer wind storms. Children develop sores and rashes that stay for weeks.

The fishermen, with the support of some environmental and church groups in the Philippines, have been trying for years to get Marcopper to stop dumping the mine tailings into Calancan Bay. With Ferdinand Marcos as a major shareholder, the residents were not very successful in getting help from the former government. When Corazon Aquino took over as President in February 1986, the islanders hoped that she would be more sensitive. But the issue has gotten tied up in bureaucratic red tape and government reorganization. Marcopper continues to dump wastes into the Bay.

Canadian churches became involved through the Taskforce on the Churches and Corporate Responsibility. Members of the Taskforce held meetings with senior management of the Canadian co-owner of Marcopper, Placer Development Ltd. The churches tried to push the company to accept more responsibility for the polluting of Calancan Bay. At a minimum, the churches argued for an independent study to determine the extent of the damage to the environment and to the livelihoods of the residents. The company has not yet agreed.

There are many other horror stories about companies polluting the environment in Third World countries. Part of the blame rests with the governments of those countries, who ignore the environmental problems in exchange for economic investment. But multinational companies are guilty of the most blatant ethical neglect in refusing to assume any more responsibility than is required by law. They have even lobbied to reduce those minimal regulations further. This provides another reason for the Third World's resentment of our power.

What we can do

As in our own country, decisions regarding economic planning in the Third World have often ignored environmental implications. Projects have been assessed primarily on their capacity to generate money, create jobs, and stimulate further economic development. Many of those projects do have positive short-term economic benefits. But the long-term impacts can be devastating.

Canada has started to look at environmental impacts when it considers supporting development projects in the Third World. The Canadian International Development Agency (CIDA) now includes some environmental criteria in their assessment of projects. But the process has several significant weaknesses. The criteria themselves are not very rigorous. CIDA often does not gather the data itself, but rather relies on the proponent of the project. That is not a very reliable way to get independent and accurate information. Nor is there adequate monitoring of projects, to determine what environmental effects were caused by a project, and to incorporate those learnings in future planning.

Voice our concerns to CIDA and government officials
Canadian foreign aid through CIDA comes from public funds. We have a right and a responsibility to ask questions

and to ensure that concern for the environment plays a bigger role than it has in the past. We can voice our concerns directly to CIDA, to the Minister responsible and to our own MPs.

Canada participates in a variety of international funding agencies that channel money from many different countries to developing nations. Two of the larger agencies are the World Bank and the Inter-American Development Bank. Countries supporting these international agencies provide funds to them; in return, each supporting country has an executive director sitting on the board that approves loans.

Those agencies are starting to become more sensitive to environmental considerations. But such factors still do not carry much weight. However, the agencies are political bodies; the directors are appointed by their own country, and have to vote according to the policies of their government. We could press the Canadian government to establish policies which would *require* our director on those boards to give significant weight to environmental considerations in assessing of project proposals. If enough countries did the same, we could have a major effect on the way projects are funded. The long-term implications for the environment would become more significant. The present and future needs of the people in the countries supported would be given more importance than short-term economic gains.

Remember, these large international lending institutions have not been particularly sympathetic to popular movements in Third World countries. Ordinary people are rarely consulted about developments that go on around them. We must push for changes in the kinds of criteria used by these institutions to decide on projects. But we must also be critical about ways that the international financial community exercises excessive power over the policies of many of the economically strapped Third World countries.

Not only governments provide development assistance to Third World countries. A great deal of work is sponsored and supported by non-governmental organizations (NGOs). The churches are among the biggest NGOs. The involvement that we ourselves have must also be guided by strong principles of concern for the long-term sustainability of the environment. Many projects have been initiated by the indigenous churches of the countries. The plans may therefore be sensitive to the needs of the local people, but neither we nor the local churches have always been fully aware of the long-term consequences. If we criticize government-funded projects, we had better be sure that our own involvement does not create more problems than it solves.

Inquire about companies' attention to the environment
In addition to our government and NGOs, many Canadian companies have parts of their operation in different countries. They are attracted by the availability of natural resources, less expensive labor, or access to markets.

Minimizing costs and maximizing profits have become the primary criteria for many business decisions in today's highly-competitive global economic system. In such a situation, companies can easily disregard the needs of a vulnerable environment. It has, after all, no voice to protest. Similarly, the well-being of the people dependent on that environment is often ignored, because these people are poor and have little political clout. Governments in many Third World countries are often struggling so hard to survive that they cannot act as vigorous protectors of the long-term health of the environment or their people.

Many companies that operate in Third World countries are based in industrialized nations like our own. In a sense, they are an extension of ourselves. We bear some responsibility for the way that they function. It is not a political responsibility like our relationship to our government. But it is at minimum a moral responsibility, since these companies are part of the economic system from which we benefit. Many are accountable to Canadian shareholders.

We can exercise some responsibility for their international

activities. It is a simple process to write to a company inquiring about whether it gives active consideration to the environmental consequences of its operations. We can go further and register objections to activities when we know they have destructive effects on the environment and/or the people.

The churches in Canada have raised these kinds of concerns through meetings with senior management of companies, attendance at their annual meetings, and filing of shareholder resolutions. As individuals and congregations, we can support and encourage our churches in these activities. We can also become involved ourselves, as individual shareholders. You do not have to own a great many shares of a company to have the right to ask questions or express opinions at its annual general meeting.

Resources for further information

Bankrolling Disasters—International Development Banks and the Global Environment, Sierra Club, Washington D.C., 1986.

Energy and Development—Planning for Growth and Conservation, edited by Moyra Tooke, a resource of the Common Heritage Programme, Teachers' Press Ltd., Ottawa, 1987.

Environment and Development—A Critical Stocktaking by David Runnals, North-South Institute, Ottawa, 1986.

In the Name of Progress—The Underside of Foreign Aid by Patricia Adams and Lawrence Solomon, Energy Probe Research Foundation, Toronto, 1985.

In the Rainforest by Catherine Caufield, Pan Books Ltd., London, England, 1986.

A logo from theWorld Council of Churches symbolizes justice, peace and the integrity of creation. We must observe all three elements.

The Future
Changing our theology, lifestyle and economics

The previous chapters of this book describe a pretty bleak picture. We are poisoning the land, the waters and the skies. There are some actions we can take. But is it too little, too late?

To turn things around, we are going to have to make many changes. This will involve changes in how we see God's creation and our relationship to it. We will have to make changes in our personal and family lifestyles. We can influence political and economic changes that affect the environment.

There are different perspectives among people about how we can make these necessary changes in our way of living. Some argue that we have to totally revolutionize our way of thinking and living. Others feel that we can alter our present approaches sufficiently without dramatically changing the way we live. What *everyone* agrees on is that we have to start making changes and making them now.

A faith that sustains the earth

In chapter 2, I discussed some ways in which traditional Christian theology has contributed to a mindset that allows our society to exploit and pollute the earth in the name of progress. I suggested some newer understandings that could help us, as Christians, protect this fragile creation that God has given us. To recognize that God loves this creation should impel us to treat it with respect. Scripture gives us some models, like that of the steward, which we can use to shift our concepts of relationship between humanity and the rest of creation. If we understand ourselves as being *part* of that creation, then we can learn how to live *with* it, in humility and mutual interdependence. Living with the rest of creation includes learning to live with the rest of humanity in a just and equitable way.

These new approaches can be given extra power if we look at some new approaches to our relationship to God. God sustains life, both ours and all other living things. God did not just create the world at one point and then leave it on its own. God is involved in on-going creation. "Creating," then, includes the concept of "sustaining."

An important historical sideline about the writing of the books we call the Bible might help us understand better what it means to see God as the sustainer of life. Because the creation story in Genesis comes at the beginning of the Bible, we often think of it as the earliest conception by the Israelite people of the nature of God.

In fact, the creation story came quite late in the development of Hebrew thought. The Israelites' real understanding of God began with their liberation from slavery in Egypt. The Exodus story is the foundation of Jewish faith. Their identity as a people, and their religion, began to develop after this historical event. As they tried to explain for themselves the world around them, they wrote the creation story. Observing the Sabbath as a day of rest, usually assumed in our time to be based on God's day of rest after six days of creation, originates in fact from the Exodus experience: "You shall remember that you were a servant in the land of Egypt, and the Lord your God brought you out thence with a mighty hand and an outstretched arm; therefore the Lord your God commanded you to keep the sabbath day" (Deuteronomy 5:15 RSV).

The Exodus story reflects the consciousness of a people aware that they have been freed from oppression by their God. They see themselves as being loved and valued by God. The concept of covenant formalizes this relationship. God promised to care for and protect the people of Israel; in exchange, the Israelites swore to honor God as the only true god and to obey God's commandments. Because God loved them, they assumed certain responsibilities.

The concept of covenant was then built into a number of other Old Testament stories. These stories are central to grasping the kind of relationship that God intended us to have with the rest of creation.

The first one, of course, is the Genesis account of creation. The book of Genesis was written after the book of Exodus. The creation account in Genesis is the way in which the Israelites explained for themselves the origin of the earth, based on their own experience and relationship with a liberating God. The characteristics of this relationship—and hence of the creation story—are love, freedom, covenant and responsibility.

So, in the Genesis story, God created the earth out of love. Each new element complemented the rest. The light and the darkness, the dry land and the waters, the vegetation, the birds, the fish and the animals were all woven into an interdependent family. Adam and Eve were created to provide companionship and love to each other. They were placed in a garden that would nourish them and meet all their needs. God looked at creation, saw that it was very good, and loved it. God gave Adam and Eve responsibility to care for all the elements of the garden.

Through creation, Adam and Eve (and by extension, the Israelite people) entered into a special relationship with God that included a covenant relationship of rights and responsibilities. Sin comes into the world through breaking this covenant relationship.

Another major Old Testament story dealing with the covenant between God and creation is the account of Noah and the flood. (In this story, as in the creation story, we should concentrate on its theme, not on the details. The point is not whether Noah took two of every species, or seven of some—or even how big a boat he would need to accomplish this purpose. The point is the purpose—to take enough of all forms of life so that they can continue that life.)

Out of frustration with the endless wickedness and violence of the people, God decided to destroy all. God "regretted having made man on the earth, and his heart was grieved" (Genesis 6:6, Jerusalem Bible). But God was pleased with one family, and so God asked Noah to build an ark so that he, his family, and *every* species could be spared. Then the floods came.

After the flood, God re-established a covenant with Noah and all creation. Never again would all the earth be destroyed by flood because of the wickedness of humanity. God applies this covenant to all creation: "I establish my Covenant with you, and with your descendants after you; also with every living creature to be found with you, birds, cattle and every wild beast with you: everything that came out of the ark, everything that lives on the earth." (Genesis 9:9–10, Jerusalem Bible)

Instead of destroying the earth, God makes a commitment to sustain it with the life-giving elements of creation: "As long as earth lasts, sowing and reaping, cold and heat, summer and winter, day and night shall cease no more." (Genesis 8:22 Jerusalem Bible)

Both the story of creation and the story of the flood were written after the Israelites had been sustained by God in the desert on their way to the promised land. They had come to know God as a source of constant support; they had come to see themselves as dependent upon a just and loving God. The creation and flood stories in this context are not really concerned with trying to explain the origins of the world. Rather, these accounts attempt to describe the dependence of humanity and all creation on God. God was responsible for establishing life in its many forms in the first place, and for sustaining that life through all time.

I believe that this perception provides the foundation for a theology that leads us directly to a caring attitude toward the earth, with whatever changes that implies for our attitudes and lifestyles, individually and as a civilization. If we truly see ourselves and the entire earth as dependent upon a just and loving God who creates and sustains all life, we will want to respond.

God has made the most generous possible covenant—to create, liberate and sustain humanity as an integral part of all creation. In response to such an expression of love, we will find ourselves choosing to care for life and all creation. We will be compelled by this persistent love to protect and nurture the earth and all that dwells therein.

Making changes to our theology is not a dull, intellectual exercise. It is profoundly spiritual. In discovering how much God loves all of creation, we learn to love it too. We get glimmers of how we are united with nature, not just as biophysical creatures, but in spiritual ways. The native peoples teach us much about this unity. When we feel that spiritual bond, we start to act differently.

The World Council of Churches has provided some valuable leadership. The WCC Assembly, in Vancouver in 1983, issued a call to churches to engage in a process of "mutual commitment (covenant) for justice, peace and the integrity of creation." The third element of this focus broke new ground for churches. Justice and peace we have worked on for years; integrity of creation is the new element capturing the imagination of the WCC and its member churches.

The WCC has sponsored some events, which bring together theologians, church representatives and environmentalists to help articulate new ways of understanding our relationship to God's creation, and what we must do to protect this fragile earth. The WCC has also developed a process that should lead to churches around the world covenanting with each other to work together to protect the environment. The WCC has produced some useful worship and discussion materials.

Living in a sustainable way

Sustainable living starts at home. We can and must make changes in our personal lifestyles, if Canadian and global environmental problems are to be solved. And we can all do *something* to improve the situation.

A debate surfaces now and then about whether individual lifestyle changes can really make a difference in problems as massive as the ecological disasters we face. Some contend that focusing on individual lifestyles is not only limited in effectiveness but can actually be counter productive. They make a valid point. Too exclusive an emphasis on individual change can diminish attention and pressure on corporations and governments. These large institutions have the power to change their policies and practices, with dramatic effects on

improving environmental quality. But experience teaches us
that they rarely take such steps willingly. Anything that
diverts energy from citizen pressure for such systemic
changes betrays our commitment to protecting the earth.

In that sense, I agree that focusing on individual lifestyle
changes can run a risk. Systemic changes, as a society, are
most important. Every chapter of this book has described
some of those needed changes.

But to concentrate only on major changes to corporate and
government policy and practice also runs a risk. Focusing
only on the systemic level and not at all on the individual
level would be a serious mistake for several reasons.

First, if we think of protection of the environment as
exclusively a responsibility of government and industry, we
will see little that we as individuals can do. Not having a
personal involvement, our commitment to doing something
about the ecological crisis will be minimal. We will have little
motivation to keep up sustained pressure on government and
industry. Without that pressure, they in turn will feel less
compulsion to act. The earth will continue to suffer.

So systemic change must be fuelled by personal change.

Second, the way our society functions is determined in
many ways by our individual lifestyles. Manufacturers put
products in unnecessarily large packages because we as
consumers buy those packages. If we as consumers stopped
making purchasing decisions by what catches our eye on the
shelf, we could compel manufacturers to cut down on wasteful packaging.

As individuals and families, we could similarly force
changes in our society by being more energy conscious, by
insisting on food products free of potentially harmful preservatives, and by refusing to use products based on environ-
mentally-destructive chemicals.

Personal change leads to systemic change.

Third, the cumulative total of our individual lifestyle
decisions certainly contributes to the health of the environ-

ment. If each household casually tosses all of its wastes into the trash can, our communities will have major garbage disposal headaches. On the other hand, if by common practice we reduced the amount of waste that we produced in the first place, and recycled as much of the remaining as possible, we would dramatically alter our whole community's waste disposal needs. Everyone would win. The environment would be better protected. New jobs would be created in recycling. Taxes for garbage collection costs could be kept under better control.

In other words, individual change *is* systemic change.

Individual lifestyle changes *can* make a difference to the future health of the planet. In fact, such changes are a necessary ingredient in any survival strategy. We will never succeed in saving the planet unless we start by doing our own part.

What changes can we make in our own lives, for a safer, cleaner and healthier environment for ourselves and future generations? People's individual circumstances vary greatly. What is appropriate for some people in one part of the country may not be the right choice for others. But we each can and must do something.

Conserving energy

Our use of energy is a major source of pollution. The cars and trucks that we drive emit harmful gases. Coal-burning generators that produce electricity contribute to acid rain. Nuclear plants create radioactive wastes we still don't know how to dispose of safely. Many types of gases are emitted through our use of energy in manufacturing. In the atmosphere, these gases contribute to the greenhouse effect and destroy the ozone layer.

In the early '70s, we heard a lot of talk about the "energy crisis." This was primarily a concern about the limited supply of oil. Because of political tensions in the Middle East, the price of oil skyrocketed. Energy conservation became fashionable. Homes were insulated more effectively. We bought smaller, more energy-efficient cars.

But the price of oil has fallen since those days. Now there is a widely held impression that we have an infinite supply of energy resources. That is wrong. The amount of non-renewable energy sources is limited. Our society's attitude says, "Make a buck now, and let tomorrow worry about tomorrow."

There still is a need to be much more energy conscious, as part of our stewardship of the earth's resources for future generations. But added to this argument for conservation is a new awareness of how much damage energy production and use does to the environment. Just because we know how to extract oil, gas or coal from some reserve, doesn't mean that we should. Our wasteful and polluting energy practices have to be curtailed, if the earth is to be saved.

There are big ways and small ways in which we can use less energy:

- limit unnecessary use of electrical appliances and only buy the most energy-efficient ones
- make sure that we turn off lights and other energy-using products when not needed
- use public transportation and car pools whenever possible; avoid driving cars alone
- insulate homes to the maximum to conserve on energy consumption for winter heating and summer cooling
- use the appropriate type of energy for specific purposes (for instance, natural gas is more efficient than electricity for heating homes)
- wherever possible, use renewable energy sources for home or farm, such as solar panels, wind power, and methane gas from compost.

Handling of toxic chemicals and hazardous wastes

We use many toxic substances in our everyday lives: household cleaners for ovens, floors and toilets; paint and paint thinner; metal and furniture polish; pesticides, fertilizers and weed killers; anti-freeze, batteries.

We have to be much more careful how we dispose of these containers and their contents. If we include them in the regular garbage, they will end up in landfill sites where they can leak and contaminate both land and water.

These substances must be recognized as poisonous, and treated accordingly. Some municipalities now have special collection facilities for hazardous household wastes. Find out what arrangements have been made in your area, *and make use of them*. Encourage your neighbors to do the same. Your health could be affected by their carelessness.

If there are no programs in your area for handling hazardous household wastes, then you can do something about it. Start researching the subject, so that you can speak knowledgeably. Then get on the phone to your local municipal councillor. Write to your newspaper. Enlist the help of environmental groups. And get yourself a collection and/or recycling facility.

At a more basic level, we should be looking for safer alternatives to hazardous products. Much of the cleaning we do around the house can be done safely and effectively using such readily available substances as vinegar, baking soda and ammonia. For a good all-purpose cleaner, combine 1/2 cup ammonia, 1/2 cup white vinegar, 1/4 cup baking soda and 1/2 gallon of water. (A word of warning: never mix chlorine bleach with ammonia or vinegar. Such combinations produce deadly gases.)

A solution of baking soda removes most of the grease in the oven. Sprinkle stubborn spots with dry baking soda, and let sit for 15 minutes before scrubbing with a damp cloth.

Some environmental and consumer groups are starting to produce guides that suggest safer alternatives to many hazardous household products. Check in your area. Also talk to your parents or grandparents. They got along without many of the modern consumer products that have made our lives both easier and more hazardous. Some natural products from their era could prove as effective and much less dangerous.

Using less, recycling more

Though the industrialized countries have only about 20% of the world's population, we consume over 80% of the earth's resources. Such consumption is unjust and inexcusable, no matter what fancy rationalizations we come up with.

I am convinced we could find ways to use less energy and to buy fewer unnecessary products. Our standard of living will not be seriously jeopardized. In fact, the quality of our lives would improve. As the health of the environment around us improves, so would our own health.

We could also recycle valuable products and substances that we do make use of. The throw-away society has got to be turned around. Each of us as individuals can do our part through the purchasing and disposal decisions that we make. By becoming serious about this in our daily lives, we can avoid further contamination of our environment and slow the use of the earth's non-renewable resources.

Recovering the health of the earth will require a fundamental shift in the mentality of our society. Society is made up of people. Us. If we start changing our own attitudes and practices, we will influence others around us.

We will also then have the understanding and credibility to challenge the more systemic policies and practices that affect how our society operates.

Tackling the big questions and the big players

This earth is doomed without some big changes. Our present industrial, agricultural and resource development practices will certainly destroy human life as we know it, and most other life forms as well, unless we change them. Even if we all were to make significant individual lifestyle changes, the earth would still be poisoned to death by the *big* polluters.

They have to be stopped. We have to stop them.

Economics controls our society. The major goal of most people, most companies and most governments is to increase their wealth. Sometimes the increase in wealth is a means to improve people's standard of living. Sometimes it is an end in itself. Concern about the *quality* of life rarely comes into the equation.

Economics does not care about the well-being of the earth. It is only concerned with how a resource can serve to increase wealth. The environment, as a concern in itself, does not exist.

Many economic decisions are based on short-term criteria. What will increase wealth the most, and most quickly? Anything that costs money with no early financial return is viewed with skepticism. Protection and preservation of the environment does have economic payoffs—but they are mainly long-term. Economic and political decisions lack such patience.

Issues related to concerns other than the direct increase in wealth have chronically had a hard time getting consideration. Unions and social activists fought for years for improved worker safety. But industries and governments had to be pushed to make any health and safety improvements that cost money and reduced profits. Environmental concerns face similar difficulties. The idea of conducting business with proper consideration for the environmental consequences of economic decisions has not up until now generated much enthusiasm in corporate boardrooms. Such considerations could slow down development, and limit or even close some profitable operations.

Yet we have an earth struggling to survive years of pollution and exploitation. All kinds of problems threaten the future. We are already experiencing the consequences of acid rain, toxic wastes, the greenhouse effect, the depleting ozone layer, radioactive wastes and a mounting garbage crisis. Almost everyone realizes that something has to be done.

But on the other hand, we live in a world where unrestricted economic growth is a god that seemingly cannot be questioned. Our economic systems are more than the sum total of the individuals working in them. These systems have forces and dynamics that reward the short-sighted and profithungry, and penalize those taking a longer view. Under our present economic system, individuals and companies feel that they cannot exhibit greater concern about the environment. They believe such action would undermine profitability, and the competition would take over.

No matter what the ideological basis for these economic systems, capitalism or communism or anything in between, unrestricted economic growth remains the unchallengeable priority. Communist countries experience just as serious environmental problems as capitalist countries. Eastern Europe has been particularly devastated by industrial pollution. In Poland, chemical contamination has left a quarter of the soil unfit for food production, and only one percent of the water is now safe to drink.

Developing countries are not spared their share of environmental problems. As chapter nine pointed out, developing countries are starting to find that some of their large-scale resource and agricultural projects have devastating ecological consequences. To bring their countries out of the poverty that oppresses so much of their population, they welcomed anything that might stimulate economic growth. But as in industrialized countries, this commitment to economic growth has pushed concern for the environment to a back seat.

How do we deal with such a situation? How can we fight such powerful economic forces? For me, the answer lies in three parts.

First, *we have to remember that we are not alone. We live in God's world.* We have the promise of the constant presence of God. The same God who created this earth is ever with us. That God not only originated the world but sustains it as well. After the great flood many centuries ago, God promised never to destroy the earth again. God continues to love the earth.

If we have faith and share God's love of this earth, then no forces are too great for us to challenge. We can call upon God to give us the wisdom, courage and perseverance we need for the struggle that lies ahead of us.

Second, *we have to make protection of the environment a primary value for our society.* No person, government or company can credibly argue that preservation of the earth doesn't matter. Some may contend that there is no need, yet, to shift our priorities from producing wealth to protecting the environment. However, an ever-increasing amount of irrefutable evidence indicates that many of our present consumer, industrial and agricultural practices threaten the future of the earth.

As such evidence accumulates, it will become impossible to dismiss it. The general public is already convinced of some need for fundamental changes. They will start demanding more change with their voices, votes and actions. The economically and politically powerful will find their positions increasingly threatened by such change.

The powerful use a kind of emotional blackmail with considerable effectiveness. They deflect pressure to change with their threat that environmental protection measures will cost jobs.

But the jobs versus environment argument will not stand up much longer. If the environment goes, so will all jobs. Certainly, a commitment by our society to environmental protection will cause some *shifts* in employment patterns. Some polluting companies may have to close. More likely, however, these companies will be able to find the money to install pollution controls, to clean up their manufacturing processes and to deal appropriately with their wastes and emissions. Some jobs will change, but there will not be a serious loss in employment.

INCO, until now the single greatest source of acid rain-causing emissions in North America, found that as it cleaned up its operations, very few jobs were lost. Their improvements not only helped the environment, they increased the efficiency of their smelters.

A societal commitment to protecting the environment will lead companies to operate in a cleaner and more sustainable way. New jobs will be created that have to do with environmental clean-up and protection.

A basic principle says that polluters should pay for cleaning up their operations. Someone who has made money for years, at the environment's expense, should pay for cleaning up that environment. That should be our basic standard. Some companies can, however, make a case that the environmental protection called for is financially impossible. A number of surveys over recent years have indicated Canadians' willingness to use tax dollars to protect the environment. People see very few reasons justifying an increase in taxes. But the future of the environment is sufficiently important to Canadians that they are willing to put their money behind it.

Third, *we have to incorporate environmental considerations as a fundamental aspect of all of our economic planning.* The new phrase describes this approach is "sustainable development." Without a commitment to sustainable development, life on earth is doomed. With sustainable development, the environment can become healthier and the relationship among the peoples of the earth can be more just.

The concept of sustainable development was given a big push in 1983. That year, The United Nations established The World Commission on Environment and Development. The Prime Minister of Norway, Gro Harlem Brundtland, was asked to chair the Commission. She was asked to take on this challenge partly because she was the only political leader who had served as a minister of the environment before becoming a head of government. She knew a lot about the ecological crises facing the world; she also had experience with the political obstacles that often prevented corrective action. The Commission was made up of members from around the world experienced in environmental issues, politics, industry, economics, agriculture, science and technology. For three years, they held public hearings around the world. They received submissions from hundreds of voluntary organizations, governments, industries and ordinary citizens. Their report, *Our Common Future*, may well be one of the most important books published in decades.

Our Common Future argues that concern about the future of the environment and the need for economic development must go hand-in-hand. The Commission members recognized clearly that we cannot call a halt to economic growth and concentrate all our energies on cleaning up the environment. That approach would lock the world's population into its present unjust pattern of distribution of resources and opportunities. The poorer countries of the world need a chance to grow economically, and to help their people out of poverty, hunger and disease. But their growth and the economic lives of the wealthier countries must be managed in a sustainable way, "to ensure that it meets the needs of the present without compromising the ability of future generations to meet their own needs."

Sustainability is the key. The pace and direction of development can be changed, so that the resources on which we depend are neither exhausted nor polluted to death, but rather are used to ensure the long-term health of the planet. The report looks at changes that are needed in economic systems, population growth, food resources, measures to protect threatened species, energy, industry, urban expansion, and common resources like the oceans and the atmosphere.

I have a few reservations about this report. I think that it could have done more in analyzing when further economic growth is good and when it is not. In many developing countries, an improved quality of life depends on a higher standard of living. To provide food, clean water, health care and education, these countries need freedom from the economic crisis which presently burdens them. Much of their hardship is linked to the massive debts owed to banks and international financial institutions controlled by the industrialized countries.

However, in our country and most others in the industrialized world, a higher standard of living does not necessarily translate into an improved quality of life. The opposite may be true. We produce ever more consumer products, developing new chemical compounds to make our life "easier" and expanding our capacity to create more energy to fuel this lifestyle of ours. Precisely these kinds of activities have so many side-effects which destroy our environment.

We need to take a much more rigorous look at appropriate and sustainable economic development. Along with environmental protection, just and equitable sharing of the earth's resources needs to be an important criteria for our future planning.

Another concern with the report is that it still emphasizes protecting the environment so that it can better meet the needs of humanity. A contribution that I think we can make is to raise the value and rights of nature for its own sake. God cares for every little sparrow. Shouldn't we?

Even with those reservations, I think that *Our Common Future* is required reading for everyone concerned about the survival of the earth. It raises some big red flags about our present way of operating in the world. It suggests some alternate approaches. And it has caught the attention of many people and governments around the world.

Canada was one of the first countries to take this report seriously. The federal and provincial governments formed a Task Force on Environment and Economy made up of politicians and representatives of environmental groups, industry, labor and academia. Though the Canadian Task Force report suffers from some of the same limitations as *Our Common Future,* it also shares its great strengths. For the first time, people are acknowledging that environmental considerations must be integrated into economic planning.

The future of the earth depends on it.

As Christians, we can reform our theology and contribute to society a new appreciation for the sacredness of all of creation. As individuals and collectively, we can change the way that we live so that instead of destroying the earth, we help it to thrive, today and for future generations to come.

Are you ready to commit yourself to this challenge?

Resources for further information

Resource Materials on *Justice, Peace and the Integrity of Creation* from the World Council of Churches, JPIC Office, P.O.Box 66, 1211 Geneva 20, Switzerland

Environmental Challenges—Learning for Tomorrow's World, edited by Paul Wilkinson and Miriam Wyman, The Althouse Press, University of Western Ontario, 1986

Environmental Ethics: Philosophical and Policy Perspectives, edited by Philip Hanson, Institute for Humanities, Simon Fraser University, 1986

Our Common Future, The World Commission on Environment and Development, Oxford University Press, 1987

State of the World—1988, A Worldwatch Institute Report on Progress Toward a Sustainable Society , Lester Brown et al., Norton & Co., 1988

Report of *The National Task Force on Environment and Economy*, Canadian Council of Environment and Resource Ministers, 1987